Out there somewhere
a shrine for the old ones,
the dust of the old bones,
old songs and tales.
    -- Gary Snyder

It is a child that sings itself to sleep.
The mind.
    -- Wallace Stevens

AM STOPPING MY FINGER NOW...

'Pure magic! The humble, genuine and skillful teacher, Mark shares the pith of his many years teaching Dharma to seasoned meditators and curious newcomers alike. Bite size morsels of delightful prose become encounters with reality, love, death, and what it means to be fully human from the Buddhist perspective free of dogma and highfalutin' philosophy. Easily related to, touching, playful and memorable. Bravo! Encore!'
    -- **Dr. Miles Neale**, *NYC, Buddhist psychotherapist, Assistant Director, Nalanda Institute for Contemplative Science*

'Mark Winwood shares the tough news that there are no short cuts on the spiritual path -- and the good news that the path "grows more beautiful and empowering with each step." He doesn't "traffic in reassurances" but walks with us through the real life of cities and trees, beaches and assisted living facilities, work and family, students and teachers, human and non-human.

    Winwood's book is about Buddhist practice, but he doesn't wander in philosophical circles or mislead with exotic entertainment. He invites us to engage the real work of cooling the "fever of fear... that comes from exaggerated self-cherishing" and stepping up to care for the relationships of which our lives are made. By sharing his "gratitude born of awareness" of this impermanent, interdependent world, and doing it with extraordinary, everyday stories, Mark does us a favor. Enjoy!'
    -- **George Draffan**, *Seattle, WA*
    Executive Director, Northwest Dharma Association

'Mark shares his remarkable didactic skills to make a simple exquisite series of easily accessible writings available to those who are eager to have their hearts and minds filled with Tibetan Buddhism. His clarity and attunement to the path resonates in his vignettes, parables and observations. Truly a pied piper for anyone who wants to grow.'
  -- **Alton Koren**, *Woodstock, NY/Orlando, FL*
    Kirtankara (Kirtan leader)

'The Dharma teachings weave their way, thread by thread, throughout these musings, creating a rich tapestry illustrating the multi-colored maze of ancient teachings blooming in twenty-first century Western life. Drawing on history, nature, wildlife, human experience, art, literature, music, myth, imagination and humor, Mark joyously shares its delight in the inter-connection of all beings . . . beautiful indeed.'
  -- **Mary Acquino**, *Mt. Dora, FL*
    (a long-time Western wanderer, who finally found her true refuge in the Dharma)

ABOUT THE AUTHOR

Mark Winwood founded the Tibetan Buddhist study/practice group The Chenrezig Project in his living room in the quiet Central Florida hamlet of Yalaha in 2005. He did so following the first of several trips to Asia, specifically India and Nepal, during which he was introduced to the Tibetan practices. The ensuing years have been filled with deepening study and practice, and the sharing of the Dharma to a diverse collection of individuals consisting of the merely curious, those deeply experienced, and all in-between.

Mark served as an adjunct professor of Tibetan Buddhism in the University of Central Florida system (Lake-Sumter State College) and is currently on the staff of the Hindu University of America, sharing Buddhist perspectives and philosophies with students pursuing advanced degrees in the Vedic studies. In Florida he shared specific applications of the Dharma with groups as diverse as high school students, diabetics and hospice nurses and volunteers.

He currently lives and shares the Dharma in the Seattle area, both in-person at his home in Snohomish County and at public venues in and around the Redmond/Bellevue area. He also hosts a weekly online gathering.

A one-time New York City newspaper publishing editor, executive and entrepreneur, he continues to "scratch the writing itch" with an internationally distributed weekly Buddhist-oriented newsletter. *Am Stopping My Finger Now* is his first book.

www.ChenrezigProject.org
mwinwood@chenrezigproject.org

Am Stopping My Finger Now...

Tibetan Buddhist musings for Western life

Mark Winwood

Copyright © 2016 Mark Winwood.
All rights reserved. No part of this book may be reproduced or utilized in any form or by any means, electronic or mechanical, including photocopying, recording, or by information storage and retrieval system, without written permission from the author.

ISBN 978-0-692-72487-3

Published by Mark Winwood
Woods Creek, Washington USA

First Edition
Printed in USA

Cover photo:
In the Cascades by Kathy Adams

For Kathy-la,
without whom this book,
and so much of me, could not exist.

Preface

This book is a collection of writings, culled from more than a decade of Dharma studies, practices and the sharing of these insights and perspectives to people of varying interests and experiences with Tibetan Buddhism.

The title is not of my own invention, it comes to us from a Tibetan man named Ngawang Singhi, who you will read about in the first chapter of this book, titled *The Brothers*. Often, Singhi and I would communicate by chatting or e-mailing with each other, me at home in Florida, he in an Internet shop in Dharamsala (India).

Singhi had learned English after arriving in India as a refugee from Tibet 15 years ago and he struggled both with the language and writing it (actually, hunting and pecking it) on a computer keyboard. Yet, his e-mails were so sweet and kind . . . and he would always end with an expression of love and his sign-off: "Am stopping my finger now."

As this book contains writings culled over five years from our weekly Chenrezig Project newsletter, each of which in an appreciative nod to Singhi ends with his words, "Am stopping my finger now," I couldn't title it anything else.

• • •

It is a pleasure and an honor to share these writings with you. To compile a list of those who contributed to my growth, and therefore the content of this book, would be to offend altogether too many whose names I would surely exclude, not by intention but because I could not make the list appropriately comprehensive. Certainly all – past and present -- who shared themselves in Chenrezig Project teachings and events are included . . . many thanks . . . organic in nature, often energetic like wild hair, our times together could not have occurred without your participation, vitality and support.

The Buddha taught that it takes many drops of water to fill a bucket, and therefore every drop matters. This is a metaphor for our lives: the Dharma path is a life-long one, and everyone we encounter plays a contributing role, even if it is not obvious at the time. To all my gratitude and appreciation.

Special thanks for the love and richness of my children: James, Anna, Emily, Wils, Claire and John and the grandchildren, Paige and Zoe. Thanks to their moms for all they've done in raising such wonderful people.

Thanks to Brother Jeff, to Jason, Sarah and their kids Ava and Charlie Rainbow. Deep gratitude to precious friends such as Sidney (aka Siddo), Bernie, Danny and those of the Florida "gang" – the Dharma peeps whose energies and love are in blossom within all that is written here.

Of course, endless gratitude to the "Professionals" – His Holiness the Dalai Lama, Lamas Yeshe and Zopa and the brilliant lineage lamas and nuns who so beautifully and perfectly preserve and share the Dharma and its preciousness both in the ways they live and teach it.

Thank you to editor William Hoard of the Lookbook Press of Redmond, WA for help and inspiration in getting this book done.

This book is a work of applied bodhicitta, an attempt to actively distill Tibetan Buddhist inclinations and understandings into the arena of modern Western life. There are works of straight Dharma, fantasy, satire, recollection, humor and "what if?".

I hope this collection will provoke thought and curiosity, while planting the seeds of the causes of happiness in the minds of all who read and share it.

And finally, thank you Singhi dear . . . I hope this meets with your approval.

-- Mark Winwood

Table of Contents

The Brothers • 1

A Happy Guy • 15

In the Shallows of the Skykomish • 23

Harness the Awareness • 29

La … La … La … • 35

Aware and Mindfully, Step-by-Step • 39

The Day • 45

Next Exit: Awakening! • 51

It's a World of Teachers • 57

The Hungry Self • 63

The Cape Canaveral Sutra • 71

Bo-dee-CHEE-ta • 75

She Arises … • 81

Crutches and Bell Peppers • 87

A Hint of Tibetan Juniper • 93

Semesters' End • 99

A $10 Million Question • 103

Fridge Samsara • 109

"Mani Brings Money" • 113

The UPS Sutra • 117

Mind: Past, Present and Future • 123

Emanations Everywhere • 129

"I Want to Learn How to Meditate" • 135

The Future of American Enlightenment • 141

Garden of Mind • 149

The Abbot of Ghoom • 153

The Journey Is the Prize • 161

"There's Nothing Magical About This . . ." • 167

The Natural Face • 175

The Last Yeti • 181

The Brothers

I've been asked more than once to relate the story of how I first became involved in the extraordinary mandala of living that is Tibetan Buddhism.

Outside of a vague Ram Dass-inspired interest in things Eastern in my college years in NYC, it all started for real during my first trip to India as a soon-to-be-divorced 52-year old man.

There, in McLeod Ganj, high on the ridge-top overlooking Dharamsala and northern India's Kanga Valley, I met Ngawang Singhi, a Tibetan refugee who was teaching tourists how to cook Tibetan mo-mo's (vegetable filled dumplings).

I was blogging during my travels, and wrote the following in May 2004 . . . I'd like to share it here. I apologize for its length, the truth is if there's a corollary between the length of this writing and the profound effect Singhi has had on my life, this piece would surpass the 587,287 words of Tolstoy's *War and Peace*.

The text from that time follows:

• • •

Dharamsala, India.

I've been fortunate to get to know several people here; some are fellow travelers, the others are "locals." Of the latter group is a Tibetan man who goes by the name of Singhi. We genuinely enjoy each other's company; I've eaten at his home, we trust each other, we have become friends. We enjoy talking of our lives and constantly ask each other questions. One day over tea he told me his story, and then, when I told him I had worked in publishing back in the U.S. he asked if I could let others know about him.

I think every Tibetan here has a story similar to Singhi's to tell, if not about themselves then about their mothers, fathers, aunts, uncles, brothers, sisters, etc. Almost all the Tibetans I've met on this trip, in Darjeeling, Nepal and here in Dharamsala are either direct or second-generation refugees from their homeland.

It took a few days to get the following written and we couldn't have done it without the tattered Tibetan-English dictionary we constantly referred to. Begun a week ago, Singhi and I finished it over candlelight last night, sitting at a table in the kitchen of the small apartment he shares with several others (the kitchen is also where he sleeps).

We had help from his brother and a friend who also lives there. For accuracy we consulted a faded Tibetan map to trace places and routes. We examined PRC prison release papers, Tibetan refugee identification papers and their special "refugee" Indian passports. The process provided an opportunity for Singhi and his brother Chime Lobsang to relive the past, and we shared some very solemn moments . . . while at other times laughing at our sillinesses. They were excited to be doing this.

Singhi, who has a slight (but improving, he says) familiarity with English has approved the following in the form you'll read it. He is extremely proud to be making a written public statement that others will read, and it is his wish that whoever reads this shares it with others. I've tried to keep the words his as much as possible.

My name is Ngawang Singhi, I am 28 years old and live in Dharamsala, India.

I was born in Tibet. My brother's name is Chime Lobsang, he is 27 years old. Although we come from different parents, we have known each other since we were small children, and consider ourselves to be brothers. My mother died during my childbirth.

I was born in Dagyab, and when I was 10 years old I entered the Buddhist monastery in Chamdo. My brother Chime Lobsang also joined the same monastery when he was 10.

In 1994, my brother, myself and three other monks wrote a letter that we displayed on the walls of the monastery. In it we said we wanted the Chinese to leave Tibet, and that we wished upon His Holiness the Dalai Lama a long life.

In reaction, the Chinese police hunted through the monastery searching for those who wrote the letter. When no one spoke, they could not find those who were responsible.

In 1995 we were moved to another monastery, the Magon Monastery in Dagyab. A high lama who had been in Germany, Lobden Sherap, recruited monks to come to this new monastery, in hopes that the monastery could be built up.

In 1996 there was great pressure between the Chinese Government and the Tibetan people. This was related to the Chinese kidnapping and "detaining for his safety" of the new Panchen Lama, who had been formally announced by His Holiness the Dalai Lama as the reincarnation of the 10th Panchen Lama.

The Chinese then replaced this real Panchen Lama with another of their choosing, one who would be loyal to the Chinese efforts in Tibet. This created great tension and the Chinese police announced that there could be no photographs of His Holiness the Dalai Lama or the real Panchen Lama in anyone's possession, with a penalty of 20 years in prison for offenders.

In the monastery we had a committee, and we talked of uprising, but did not. Instead, four people wrote a letter saying that we did not think it was proper to obey the Chinese order and that we urged everyone to speak up for Tibet's freedom. We were monks, we had decided to spend our lives with our Buddhist beliefs and then teaching them to others. How could the Chinese say that what was born in our hearts, and our ancestors' hearts, was criminal? The letters were stuck to the walls of the monastery in the middle of the night for all to read.

The Chinese were very angry, and the chief of Chinese police came to our monastery and each monk was ordered to complete a form, writing his name, his father's name, his place of birth and other information. The Chinese police then compared the writing on these forms with the writing on the letters, and with the help of spies in the monastery they identified and accused five monks of writing the letters. My brother and I were among them.

On October 6, 1996, we were put into the Dagyab prison by the Chinese police. We were tortured and beaten, and were shocked with electrical wires. Then we were sent to the large prison in Chamdo where we were kept in solitary confinement for four months, handcuffed and leg-cuffed. We were repeatedly beaten with clubs, but when we were taken to the office and asked by the Chinese police who wrote the letters and who supported us, and who gave us money, each of us said it was only "I" who did it and that I received no help.

The Chinese continued to beat us, with thick sticks and poles and stones, sometimes until we became unconscious. Then they would throw buckets of cold water on us to awaken us so that they could beat us some more. They were full of brutal punishment. Still, our response was "it was me, nobody else." This continued regularly.

After four months we were allowed to be removed from solitary jail and were taken outside to pick up large rocks and stones from the prison farm. It was at this time that my brother and I were each sentenced to an additional three years in Chinese prison.

As prisoners, we were assigned the task of cleaning the Chinese police toilets. It was filthy work designed to make us feel broken, and as dirty as we became we were not allowed to wash ourselves. The food we were given to eat was also dirty, and even though it was very cold, we were never given any meat to eat. Most of the time we were given boiled cabbage, the cabbage was the ones that were not good enough to be sold in market. There were bugs (cockroaches) crawling in our food. We all grew sick. And this treatment was not just for us, all prisoners, even the old ones, were treated in the same manner.

As political prisoners my brother and I were held in cells in which we were each alone. I became very ill, I had pains in my body, could not control my urine and it was difficult for me to walk. There was urine and feces all over the floor in my cell, there was no toilet provided.

On January 15, 1998, seven prisoners, including my brother and I, were sent to a new prison. The food was better but the work was harder. We did heavy labor, cut wood, sifted sand and soil and planted trees. Every day we began work before 7:00am and worked until very late at night.

After work we were forced to watch Chinese political broadcasts on television and then the police would blow a whistle and the prison lights were turned out. We were told by the Chinese that Buddhism was "not peace" and we were not allowed to pray in any manner. We were not allowed to talk or whisper, there were Chinese police hiding behind the doors to try to catch us if we did.

I continued to be very ill, there was much wrong inside of me. My brother and other prisoners would always ask the police to check on me, to put me in the hospital. They were beaten when they asked, but they did not stop asking.

One day I did get to the hospital. At the hospital I was told I could be treated with medicine if I paid 3,000 yen in advance of any treatments. I did not have any money.

The Chinese police allowed my brother, accompanied by a police, to go out of the prison and beg for money for my medicine. He did get the money from the Tibetan community.

I was given oxygen and medicine, and was still not allowed to speak to anyone as there was usually a guard at my bed. For the first week I was unconscious. After one and one-half months I began to feel a little better, and I was sent back to my prison cell. I then had to work every day even though I was barely healthy enough to be put out of the hospital.

On October 7, 1999 my brother and I were released from prison. As political prisoners, the Chinese police ordered us to ask permission if we wanted to go anyplace away from town, and permission would only be granted to visit family members. We were also ordered never to go to any monastery, and never to speak to any groups. Police in our area were alerted to watch us at all times.

So even though we were not in prison, our big problem was that we could not go anywhere. We decided that we needed to leave Tibet, our home country, to escape from the Chinese.

We received permission to visit a hospital for my bad health in Lhasa and we went there. We then began our escape. We paid 1,000 yen for papers that allowed us to travel on a bus from Lhasa to Shigatse. There we secretly boarded a truck along with 27 other people who were also seeking escape, and went to Saga. From Saga, the 29 of us walked into the Himalayas.

Our group had monks, old people and children. It was December and very, very cold in the mountains. It was windy and there was much snow. We had very little to keep us warm and some of us had ice on our eyes. Some of our group lost toes to frostbite, but my brother and I were fortunate and did not. After 25 days of walking, on January 6, 2000, we reached Nepal.

After seven days in Nepal we were put on a bus and sent to Dharamsala in India. We were received here, and everyone wanted to know about those we were in prison with. It seemed everyone knew people in Chinese prisons in Tibet.

In Dharamsala, we spent four months in the Tibetan Refugee Center. We met His Holiness the Dalai Lama, who greets all new refugees from Tibet, and were sent to school to learn English and other skills. My brother was sick and left school. I was also still sick but stayed in school for four years. There is a policy among Tibetans here that if one is not in school, one needs to be working.

Today, my brother is a cook in a restaurant here. I am working by teaching foreign visitors to Dharamsala about Tibetan cooking. I am still sick, my situation with my body is not so good. But it is better this year than it was last year. We both take medicine to try to combat the sickness we still reserve from Chinese prison.

We cannot contact anyone in Tibet because it would cause them great trouble with the Chinese government. We are very sad not to be able to speak to our families in Tibet.

Singhi, in his kitchen

It makes us angry to know how the Chinese try to make the tourist places in Tibet look good. People cannot see what is really happening in Tibet without seeing it through the eyes the Chinese have put in place.

We are not afraid of the Chinese because we will never go back to Tibet as long as it is ruled by the Chinese.

Please, whoever reads this, please try to seek out the truth and pay attention to the situation in Tibet and what is happening to the Tibetan people. Please do not listen to what the Chinese government says because it is not true.

And please understand as you read this, there are many Tibetans being tortured and punished in Chinese prisons for no reason other than because they love their home and religion. And also please remember that there are tonight Tibetans walking through the snow in the high mountains to India and Nepal trying to be free.

-- Ngawang Singhi; McLeod Ganj, India. May 8, 2004

(Writing current day, September 2014)

I had been back to Dharamsala a few times after that first visit, and always found Singhi, who was no longer teaching Tibetan cooking but was tending to a small stall selling crackers, drinks and other convenience items.

I last saw him as I was leaving Dharamsala, about to board the overnight bus to Majnu-ka-tilla, Delhi's Tibetan colony. He came to say good-bye and placed a khata around my neck, signifying his wishes for my safe trip and blessings for a happy, soon-to-occur return.

Two very different, far-away yet close friends, we renewed our agreement: that I would continue to spread the beauty of the Tibetan people and their precious Buddhist ways of being back home in the U.S., and that he would take the best of care of himself.

It's a funny thing, over the years there have been so many Chenrezig Project teachings and events including sadhanas, film festivals, meditation and other workshops, etc., and many people have expressed to me their gratitude for doing all I've done to share what I've come to learn and experience from these exquisite philosophies and practices.

The truth is, none of this would have happened if not for this lovely Tibetan man and his extraordinary openness and willingness to share his story with me, and by extension, us.

Whenever there are times where I began to feel self-important and very much the Dharma "teacher" I go back to that tiny, dimly-lit kitchen with Singhi and Lobsang and our well-used dictionary and reconnect with the sense of awe of what I had unexpectedly stumbled upon, and the immense beauty of not just Tibetan Buddhism but Buddhist Tibetans.

This is the spirit in which the Chenrezig Project originated, our stated mission "infusing Western life with Tibetan Buddhist compassion" and our guiding curriculum being Tsongkhapa's Lam-rim Chen-mo, the "Steps to Enlightenment."

Centuries of Tibetan Buddhist teachings and practices have proven this to be a direct path to the essence represented by Chenrezig . . . the mind of great compassion born of awakened

wisdom, arrived at through study, reflection/meditation and engagement in philosophies of ethics, selflessness and wisdom.

Over the years the strength of our vision has been adherence to this precious curriculum; never allowed to be confused, diluted or contaminated by any one person's grasping at or spewing off-point, self-serving ideas and notions.

Feel-good is nice but it doesn't last and is not Buddhism. There are no quick-hit, once-a-week dilettante practices that will provide any long-term benefit. (Feeding one's ego is not Dharma practice.)

We continue on, with awareness of intention ... the question "why am I doing what I am?" should pass through the mind hundreds of times each day ... we strive to answer this question with clarity and honesty, even though we might not like the answer. We try to embrace it all ... being both stern and gentle.

We gather to learn, discuss and share ourselves, with an eye toward cultivating the mind and skills most useful in helping reduce the causes of suffering of all beings, i.e., the 'great' greater good.

This is what we've done, what we do. It is the trail-head of the Bodhisattva path, clearly marked, in plain sight for those who choose to step out and see it.

It is a path that is right there in Delhi and Dharamsala, in Florida and now in Washington State ... it cuts through our bedrooms and kitchens, work places and playgrounds ... we can see it in the eyes of our children and friends, our pets and lovers and parents, as well as in strangers and those who consider us to be their enemies.

It is there, clearly marked, wherever we are and wherever we go.

We are in-service caretakers and gardeners of the Dharma to the best of our ever-expanding abilities. It is what will continue on.

It must. We owe it to Singhi, Lobsang and the Tibetan people, who have given us so very much.

• • •

The life of a Tibetan refugee is unsettled and difficult.

Currently, Singhi and I have lost touch with each other, the last we communicated he was struggling with spotty Internet access and no work in Turkey, unsure of how long he would remain there.

He remains deeply embedded in my heart, I look forward to our re-connection.

-- Am stopping my finger now, thank you for reading.
(9.19.14)

A Happy Guy

I was looking at my July calendar, to see what events are coming up ... the things to look forward to and what I need to begin planning for.

Something about the numbers stood out ... seventh month, 2015 ... and I realized we are now halfway through the year that stands at the midpoint of the 21st century's second decade.

And something about that struck me.

I'm in my 64th year now, a slow-moving man who continues to try to lose a few pounds while subtly striving to evolve through matters of the spirit, and I don't have to pretend to be anything else. I am content, quite happy actually, to continue to study and share the practical encouragements the Dharma has to offer, merging what I learn with my everyday work and continuing to discover the simple truths about what it means to love others.

In doing so I sometimes speak about Enlightenment, not that I can relate any knowledge from experience, but rather by sharing some perspectives from our teachings, influenced by guided imagination fueled by wondrous conviction.

The Vajrayana path proclaims to be one in which the emergence from ignorance into enlightenment may be achieved in a single lifetime, but I have instinctively identified with a Buddhist tale that speaks of a slightly longer time-frame.

This is the one that tells of the bird with a ribbon hanging from its beak, who once every hundred years flies above a massive mountain of granite. Each time -- again, once every hundred years -- the ribbon rubs along the mountain's summit. Once we begin on the Dharma path, explains the parable, in the time it takes the mountain to be completely eroded flat to the ground by the ribbon's rub, is the length of time it takes for the enlightened mind to be uncovered.

This teaching is one of infinitely patient diligence: we can't urge the bird to fly overhead more often, or drop some sort of rock-dissolving acid or sticks of explosives on the mountain, or ask other birds to pitch in and help.

Vast as it might be, this is the time-frame ... all we can do is continue sure-footed on the path, striving to remain clear and balanced, sure that one day its end will be reached with the perfect liberation of our mind achieved.

We do this step-by-step, moment-after-moment, lifetime-after-lifetime.

Patience indeed.

· · ·

Thinking about the passage of time, I put myself back 50 years ago... it is 1965 and I am 13 years old, growing up in New York City (Queens).

I'm in the PS 139 schoolyard with some of my friends, sitting in the shade up against the stick-ball wall. It's a hot summer day and I'm eating my favorite power lunch: a baloney hero sandwich from Tony's Deli and drinking an ice cold Yoo-hoo, the drink of champions. (Yogi Berra said it, "It's Me-he for Yoo-hoo!")

Normally we'd be talking about the Yankees and the Mets, the brash new heavyweight champion Cassius Clay or the Beatles, or the girls we're just beginning to notice in "that" way. But we'd been to the World's Fair in Flushing Meadow the day before, our hometown "World of Tomorrow" less than an hour's walk from our schoolyard, and it had tickled our fancy. So we're talking about the way we think the world might be for each of us in the year 2015, 50 years hence.

When my turn comes, it's hard to visualize 50 years into the future... year numbers no longer starting with 19... being 63 years old, a completely different person... kind of weird.

I mumble something about hoping I'll be the father of some children, and how I can't really imagine living anywhere but in New York. And then, always the wanna-be clever kid, I sum it up with a shrug, saying I really don't know what my world will be like, that I really have no idea at all what might happen...

Maybe I'll own my own private flying rocket-car, or other things equally futuristic, but all I'll really want is to be happy. Simply to be, do and have happy. Throughout my life and into my old age . . . however long my life will be . . . I just want to be a happy guy.

. . .

Here I sit today, with so much of my life having been lived. Marriages and divorces, the fathering of six uniquely wonderful children, the deaths of my parents as well as many friends and loved ones . . . extensive, often adventurous travels to remarkable places, a career with episodes of high-flying and flaming defeats, times of good health and difficult illness, financial challenges and a never-ending stream of remarkable people.

And somehow, through all the twists and turns, that goofy-clever kid's notion of just wanting to be happy 50 years in the future has come to be. Here's how:

I now understand that I have never known what tomorrow has in store, these days perhaps more than ever. Because of this I'm learning to live more fully in the enduring ebb and flow.

Nothing has an inherent essence; nothing can be counted upon to remain predictable, nothing is dependable or trustworthy or "in the bag" for any length of time.

Everything is in flux, perpetually coming together, abiding for a bit and then decaying into its falling apart. There is no destiny, no fate, no consistency, just the interplay of occurrences of which I understand I'm a part of, and have a responsibility to participate in as wisely and wholesomely as I can.

There are going to be good days and bad, easy times and difficult ones, pleasurable and not so pleasurable happenings.

And while everything is changing, what life asks of us -- actually what navigating the Buddhist path demands -- will be no different tomorrow than it is today, or was yesterday. It is simply to remain clear and balanced while knowing that we too are an interdependent aspect of all things as they are occurring, and then to work within that framework as wisely and skillfully as we can for the benefit of every sentient being.

Yes, situations change. Things come and go, and informed guidelines for navigating the Buddhist landscape abound. I have hundreds of Dharma books in my library, held together by bindings time-worn from heavy use, many of them filled with margin notes and highlighted text.

And even though I could pile them into a tower as high as the tree-tops, climb to the top and sit upon all that wisdom, at the end of the day the playing board on which genuine happiness is experienced is not in the pages of those books or in the messaging of their authors.

Rather, it is found at the base of the pile. In the nubby, granular carpet of our everyday world, where we stand on our own two feet and, understanding that self-grasping misunderstandings hold us back, work with our mind engaged for the benefit of every being that comes our way: skillfully, virtuously, compassionately ... and, through repeated practice, increasingly intuitively.

. . .

I had no hint of this, the methodologies of happiness, when I was 13 years old. I just thought it would be nice to have the pleasures of being happy, without even a curious care of what the causes leading to those pleasures might be.

I wonder what my reaction would have been 50 years ago if someone told me the Buddhist path would so effectively help guide me to the true causes of the happiness I sought.

Buddhism? Really? So foreign and exotic, who knew anything about it? My neighborhood was a solid mixture of Irish, Italian and Jewish kids, we knew no Buddhists. I probably would have dismissed the whole idea with an off-color joke, followed by a righteously disbelieving giggle.

Today, things have changed. With partial front dentures I doubt I could comfortably bite into one of Tony's semolina heroes, and if my doctor caught me drinking Yoo-hoo she'd probably drop me as a patient.

But my mind has been enriched by our profound teachings and practices. And so the giggle remains.

Aware of the ribbon continuing to brush along the mountaintop for so many travelling this path, it is now the best type of giggle ... easily arising and joyous, it is a giggle of deep happiness.

-- Am stopping my finger now, thank you for reading.
(6.18.15)

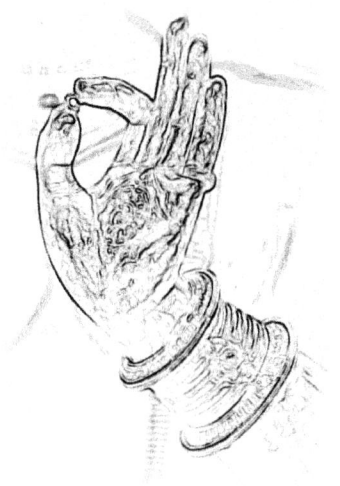

In the Shallows of the Skykomish

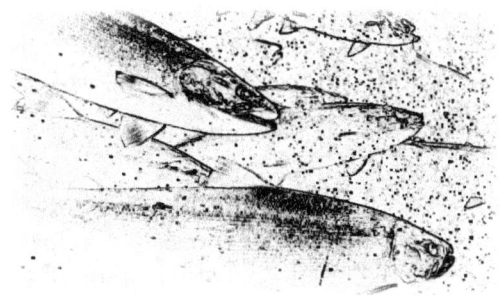

The weekend weather was beautiful.

Kathy and I went for a ride along the Skykomish River. Finding a place to stop and park, we hiked down to the river's edge, drawn toward the sound of fresh, shallow water running over stones.

The river was moving quickly, and as we emerged from the forest and approached the water we noticed something unusual: deep folds on the surface of the water, moving in the opposite direction of the river's flow . . . swirling ripples, of a different nature from those caused by eddys, water rushing over rocks or blown by breezes.

Fins were at the center of these ripples ... salmon fins. We are now in the first days of autumn, and the salmon, having returned from the sea to their natal waters, are in the river shallows, dying.

• • •

Salmon die after spawning due to exhaustion and malnutrition. This has to do with the difficult upriver migration they make, returning to their own birth place. Flipping their bodies in the air and hurling themselves against the downward flowing water is no easy feat, and is one that is energetically exhausting. To prepare for this, salmon must fully develop in the ocean and build up fat reserves.

Salmon stop feeding as they enter fresh water. Once they enter the river there is little food to eat and they stop investing in the maintenance of their bodies. As their stomach is no longer needed for digestion it begins to disintegrate internally -- leaving more room for the developing eggs and sperm. They then begin living off the stored fat that had been accumulating during their life in the ocean.

During this process their flesh begins to change; lacking flavor, becoming pale in color and mushy in texture. Most salmon used for food are caught in the ocean (before they start upstream), where they have the best flavor, color and texture.

Their upstream journey is often long and difficult, and by the time they get to the spawning grounds -- if they make it -- they have used up their stores of energy.

The river riffles are filled with them, splashing in death throes of short spurts and long curls, flipping sideways and then regaining balance, momentarily righting themselves. It is a sad to watch dance and it continues, over and over, until it ends.

. . .

We walk out on the rocky beach into the river a little bit, and there in a pool before us is a beautiful silver salmon, floating, gasping . . . still alive, but just barely.

I wonder if a vision of her life is passing before her as she lies here with her mouth stuck open and one unblinking eye staring up through the enormous trees overhead to the sunlit sky beyond.

I imagine not.

I can only suppose she has no recollection of the urges that have driven her, no recall that as a youngster she left this river to travel to the deep heart of the sea. And I suppose she cannot now remember fighting her way against the river's torrent, leaping up sunlit falls and choosing a strong mate.

Does she even know she has laid her eggs, fulfilling her role in shaping the future? Can she remotely realize that each day she lived, so many of her comrades fell to natural catastrophes and cunning predators and diseases and accidents and the nets and hooks of humanity? And, as she lies here dying, can she possibly understand that she has succeeded and survived?

One hopes so.

. . .

Kathy and I have been in Washington State for more than a year now. Upon hearing we were leaving Florida for the Northwest, many people commented on the months of cool dark, rainy winter days we'd be trading the sunny, warm Florida winters for.

Yes, and the exchange has been a good one for us.

Our first winter here was wet and at times raw. But not only wasn't it unpleasant, the cool blankets of rain and fog were calming and embracing. And we've come to learn the importance of the persistent rain on this ecosystem of which we have chosen to be a part.

Each drop of rain is a perceptual lens through which we can see the life force of this magnificent region. Raindrops build streams, and streams -- guided this way and that by the rugged contours of the land -- lead to rivers, rivers to watersheds, and those watersheds, merged together, flow to and become sea.

Along the Pacific Coast of North America -- from the California redwoods north to the Arctic Ocean -- any summertime stream that carries more than a couple of garden hoses' worth of water is probably home to at least one species of salmon.

It is in these flowing waters, which are everywhere, that the magnificent salmon -- symbolic of the wild and free beauty of the Pacific North -- are born and return to spawn . . . planting new life . . . fulfilling their responsibility, continuing the process.

And then when their work is done, exhausted, they die.

. . .

The salmon in the pool at our feet slips down into the river gravel, repeatedly, until her lifeless body slowly rises, coming to rest in the current against a rock.

We are reminded that death is not always a tragedy and can be natural and right and even beautiful. In the case of the salmon, instructed by nature, death arrives when life has become complete.

Having emerged from its now useless form, her mind swims in a new freedom, unfettered by baggage of body . . . aware of a very gentle movement, vaguely forward.

Consciousness unencumbered . . . an image of a worn, lifeless carcass on the rocks . . . now irrelevant . . . a pile of left-behinds . . . food for the river scavengers.

Her mind moves through time, aware of diversions on all sides but none are alluring enough to capture its attention . . . flowing straight-ahead toward a light, perfectly clear, radiating living peace and infinite grace, comfort and safety . . . beautiful beyond description, it is all she is drawn to . . . it is everything there is.

Fearlessly, she approaches and then enters into the softly luminous glow, on the verge of rebirth . . .

-- Am stopping my finger now, thank you for reading.
(9.30.15)

(Thanks to Dr. Carl Safina for some of the salmon lore.)

Harness the Awareness

The historians tell us that Siddhartha Gautama, the historical Buddha, lived more than 2,500 years ago in Northern India.

Having uncovered the enlightened mind, he taught the path of similar achievement to others for 45 years, until his death at the age of 80.

Meaningful work, done well; obviously the Buddha and his teachings have had a far-reaching impact.

Here in the U.S., so far away in time and distance, the Buddha is a cultural icon. We see his familiar image in restaurants and beauty salons, on car bumper stickers and as lapel pins, necklace pendants and lawn ornaments.

As a Dharma practitioner, I regard the Buddha as someone quite unique: a remarkable individual who managed to realize the full potential of his mind ... a potential all sentient beings harbor. And then, brilliantly enriched with hard-earned wisdom and compassion, he set forth and shared -- using both dialog and example -- a curriculum for all other beings to do the same.

So fantastic . . . he holds a precious place in my heart.

Perhaps it is my perspectives of who and what a Buddha is that prompt me to write the following for your consideration . . .

. . .

While affirming the accomplishments mentioned above, a Buddha is also nothing special.

Within the human realm, he (or she) is a common person; the landscaper, hospital lab tech, desktop publisher, high school student, bread baker, dentist, homeless person.

He or she may be living with an incurable disease or in seemingly perfect health.

Body size, shape and color have nothing to do with it, nor does native language or most deeply felt religious beliefs. Senior citizen or toddler, serious or silly, joyous or glum, lonely or happily entertained . . . all included.

Much of the literature would have us believe that Buddhahood is a state of mind attained after eons of lives, accomplished after enduring an almost endless curlicue of karma. After all that time we finally arrive into a reality free from self-cherishing desire . . . a nirvana . . . the indescribably beautiful attainment of the enlightened mind.

It is something wonderfully difficult to achieve and completely satisfactory ... the perfect flip side from the hustle and bustle of ordinary sentient life ... another world or dimension.

My sense is that these concepts of Buddhahood as being something "beyond" are most useful at first, effective in capturing the imagination and helpful in creating motivation and intention, providing a far-off "target" to aim for.

But here's the thing, what I'm thinking. Maybe that exceptional person who was a Buddha ... is no different from us ... right now.

• • •

It's any day.

We awaken in the morning, sit for a few moments and then head to the bathroom ... shower, brush our teeth. The weather report guides us on how to dress. A cup of coffee or tea and some fruit or cereal for breakfast. Read the newspaper. Walk the dog. Think about what the day holds in store for us as we head out to work.

E-mail and phone calls, meetings, challenges. Perhaps a relaxing lunch, probably hurried. Some afternoon fatigue as work continues, then the workday ends and we head home. Dinner, maybe time spent with friends, loved ones.

Kids' homework. A bike ride. Read a chapter in the new book. Music. Facebook. Television. A few hours of "leisure" time. For many of us, time haphazardly spent thinking of what's occurring in our lives ... health, finances, relationships, vacation plans, deadlines approaching, errands needing to be run.

Moods happen ... happy, depressed, confident, worried.

Anticipation. Fear. Excitement.

Then off to bed. Set the alarm for the morning. Goodbye to the day just passed. Cool pillows. Cuddling. Dreams. Sleep. Rest.

And all this time, through all these ordinary moments . . . day after day, deep in our mind . . . deep in the nature of our mind . . . a perfect Buddha abides. Through tiny cracks in our ignorance, time and again, awakened notions arise . . . a sense of brightness, a scent of well-being, even amidst our trials and challenges . . . *especially* amidst our trials and challenges.

An unmistakable touch of joy, an extraordinary feeling of "knowing" . . . a oneness not just with life but with everything around us . . . trees, animals, people, clouds and breezes.

Something is happening. You are falling into the most wholesome kind of love -- a great love -- and you're falling into it because you're opening into an understanding of who you truly are . . . and what you're truly not.

It is a love of confidence and caring, it breathes and shines within you.

It is a love that caresses others without seeking anything in return.

You are a Buddha. We are a Buddha.

A sense of what our teachings call bodhicitta bubbles up . . . based in great wisdom and compassion it spills over, overflowing, touching everything, even your conflicts and the people you do not get along with. Problems are savored and overcome. Desperate situations become the compassionate workings of your life.

Empowering beyond words, you've never experienced anything like it. And yet it's been sitting there, just below the surface of your everyday mind, waiting to blossom.

You have awakened.

This is not science fiction or make-believe, nor is it some delusional fantasy or last gasp before going under. Neither is it something beyond us, or beyond you.

It is here. Right now.

It's here while you're doing whatever you are doing ... sipping tea, reading this, talking to a friend, remembering long-ago kisses, tuning a guitar, walking your dog, tying your shoe, smoking a cigarette, doing a crossword puzzle on an early morning NYC subway train.

It is not outside. It is inside. It is you. You are a Buddha, completely empty of any limitations you have ever placed on yourself, or accepted from others.

You are a Buddha.

Find it. Harness the awareness. Be it.

-- Am stopping my finger now, thank you for reading.
(4.03.13)

La . . .

    La . . .

        La . . .

It's often the simple things that are the sweetest.

The Tibetan language has some words and phrases that are stunning in both their beauty and ability to simply communicate complex ideas . . . and I'd like to tell you about "la."

La has different uses in Tibetan, it is most well-known to indicate a mountain pass, of which the highest in the world are located in Tibet. Some well-traveled Tibetan Himalayan passes are the Jelep-la, Nathu-la, Pang-la, Gyatso-la, Kamp-la and Serkyum-la.

Some believe that James Hilton used the Changri-la pass near Mt. Everest as the Shangri-la model for his 1933 novel *Lost Horizon*, about a fictional lamasery in the Himalayan Valley of Blue Moons, deep in Shangri-la, where peace and harmony abound.

Ironically, "Shangri" has no meaning in the Tibetan language.

Due to Hilton's book and the subsequent 1937 Frank Capra film of the same title, Shangri-la quickly came into common usage as a place where all that is good and true is preserved. Today "Shangri-la" is aggressively promoted by the state-run Chinese travel industry to embody Tibet to potential tourists. (Their promotional material refers to Shangri-la as being a Tibetan phrase meaning the "sun and moon in one's heart." This is no more true than Disney World being the place "where all your dreams come true.")

But the Tibetan "la" has an additional use, which is both lovely and fun. La is an informal honorific term which is appended to a name to indicate affectionate respect. It is similar to "ji" in Hindi and "san" in Japanese.

Why isn't there a commonly-used affectionately respectful equivalent in English?

It is very sweet and uplifting to append "la" to someone's title or name, try it out . . . Geshe becomes Geshe-la . . . Ani becomes Ani-la . . . Mary becomes Mary-la, Billy turns to Billy-la, Mom and Dad to Mommy-la and Daddy-la. Kathy-la . . . Siddo-la . . . Bernie-la . . . Em-la . . . Anna-la . . . try it with your friends, or maybe your pet . . . Diogi-la . . . your spouse or partner . . . Sweetee-la or Honey-la or Tootsie-la . . . or even your hometown . . . Seattle-la . . . Manhattan-la . . . Yalaha-la.

Public figures? Sure, why not . . . Obama-la, Dalai Lama-la . . . the Pope-la . . . Lebron-la . . . Bozo-la . . . even Trump-la or Putin-la. You get the idea.

A name with "la" added to it floats, and is sung rather than spoken, creating in the minds of both the speaker and hearer a dancing sense of friendship and respect. Light and airy, it is poetic, a soft kiss of affection. Saying it or hearing it said to you feels like a gentle embrace of well-being.

Spoken or heard, it is good for your mind.

Even if not verbalized, as a thought "la" is beneficial, a sweet way to enrich perceptions of others with a bubble of regard and warmth. And remember, mind is so fertile ... done regularly, "la" will first 'upgrade' the names, subtly infusing them with affection. Then, with familiarity, since we sentients are so good at imputing essence based on labels, you'll soon begin to enrich your intuitive perceptions of what (or who) the name represents, i.e., the "la" quality will stick to them.

And the way you actively perceive, and thereby relate to and experience people in your life will begin to change in "sweet heart" ways.

• • •

Try it ... think of people in your life, think (or say) their name, and then repeat it adding "la" as an uptick to the end ... can you hear the difference?

Do this repeatedly and mindfully, let it cross-over into your thinking of others, you may find it to be a surprisingly effective "self-and-other-softener."

You need not be Buddhist, Tibetan, or anything else ... just human-la!

There are so many precious gifts the Tibetan people have brought to us, this one -- the use of "la" joined to a name -- is beautifully simple, endlessly sweet . . . and it works.

Practice it, see for yourself.

-- Am stopping my finger now, thank you for reading. (7-3-13)

Aware and Mindfully, Step-by-Step

The teaching on the Heart of the Perfection of Wisdom Sutra had ended and the 21st Century Bodhisattva had asked those present to revisit the Sutra in the coming days until their next gathering together.

The students were filing out, notes in hand. One of the last to leave was Jeanette, a newer student who, the Bodhisattva had noticed, was sitting throughout most of the evening's teaching deep in thought.

It was no surprise when Jeanette approached, and in a serious tone asked if she could have a few words with her. The Bodhisattva smiled her assent.

"These teachings really resonate with me, even the Heart Sutra is beginning to make some sense," Jeanette related. "But I'm a little anxious, I want to understand and experience more . . . I

feel as though I need to take some giant steps ... to get myself further along to where I want to be more quickly."

With a knowing smile, the Bodhisattva replied, "Well Jeanette, Buddhism is a profound system; to study, understand and then begin to embrace and engage in these perspectives and practices is a long and winding path, and a very rich one ... you are really just at the beginning now."

"Oh, I understand and appreciate that," Jeanette said. "But even still, there must be a shortcut, a quicker way ... you know, a kind of express train that'll bypass many local stops along the way?"

The Bodhisattva experienced a moment of sadness. Understanding this exchange could be a significant one for Jeanette, she wanted to be both supportive and honest as well as empowering and kind. She thought for a few moments before responding.

. . .

"Jeanette, I hear and understand what you are asking, I sense some doubt and frustration, not uncommon for beginning Dharma students. In a way you remind me of myself years ago.

"Your question brings to mind a favorite teaching, from the great Lama Atisha in answer to a request from Jang Chub O, one of his senior students, for a conclusive "summary" teaching.

"I'll try to share the essence of Atisha's message to help you get a different 'view' of the path before you. Come sit beside me.

• • •

"First, let me say there is no 'bullet train' or 'short-cut' to the places the Dharma can or will take you, nor should there be. The Dharma path grows more beautiful and empowering with each step we take upon it. To somehow circumvent or speed-dial past its enduring wonder would be neither wise or beneficial . . . it would keep you from participating in so much, or as the Tibetans sometimes say, the richness of the experience of churning milk into sweet butter would be lost.

"So with patience we move along our path, mindful that to do so requires paying attention, for which listening is indispensable; listening to your teachers, to everything and everyone around you, and to yourself. Speed is of no use here, be patient . . . take the time to quiet down and listen . . . to hear clearly.

"And remember, while listening is essential, one cannot progress along the path by merely hearing the Dharma . . . we must take what we've heard, understand it, bring it into our practice and engage with it earnestly.

"Atisha often advised it is important that we, especially as beginners, strive to avoid situations that disturb our mind. So it is better to avoid those who cause our delusions to intensify, and to rely upon those who help us to nurture our virtues. This is especially important for us to consistently take heart in, without timetables and deadlines."

Jeanette nodded her understanding.

"And in whatever we are doing, we should watch our mind, repeatedly and mindfully dedicating our virtues throughout the day and night to the benefit of sentient beings everywhere.

"Pride and arrogance resulting from words of praise and fame serve only to beguile us. Atisha warned we should blow them away as we would blow our nose."

"Tell me more," Jeanette said softly. The Bodhisattva smiled and gently took her hand.

"Generate compassion for those you see as lower than yourself, and especially avoid despising or humiliating them.

"Do not look for faults in others, but look for faults in yourself, then purge them like bad blood.

"Speak truthfully without malice."

After moments for reflection, the Bodhisattva continued, "There's more Jeanette, but I think this is enough for now. Perhaps I can best summarize this short 'travel guide' for you with the following . . . always keep pure moral discipline in everything you do, for it leads to ongoing beauty in this life and happiness thereafter. And of course, moral discipline means non-harming intentions and actions."

Jeanette smiled broadly.

"Atisha concluded his teaching to Jang Chub O by explaining that what he had said was not only words from his mouth, but sincere advice from his heart . . . I say the same to you, Jeanette.

"If you follow these guidelines, impatient desires or needs for a short-cut or accelerated progress will fall away. Study and practice the Dharma with great attention and you'll experience results that will arise immediately, without your having to wait a very long time . . . results that will become the motivations and causes for many profound 'making progress' moments to come.

"This, dear, is how our path is best traveled."

"Yes, I understand, thank you," Jeanette gently squeezed the Bodhisattva's hand. "Time isn't really relevant. . . there's no slow path or fast path, just the path I pave for myself at my own speed and ability, aware and mindfully, step-by-step . . . what else could there possibly be?"

Jeanette and the 21st Century Bodhisattva shared a tender hug, after which Jeanette went on her way.

-- Am stopping my finger now, thank you for reading.
(9.12.12)

The Day

Wednesday, September 16 dawned cloudy and cool in Western Washington. Reports on the ongoing forest wildfires and the Seattle teachers' strike filled the local news, while the GOP debate to be held later that evening dominated the national headlines.

All in all, for most just a normal mid-week day.

But for Charlie and Olivia this day had been dreaded, and while they had seen it coming for several months, it brought a sadness deeper and more painful than any they had ever experienced or imagined.

Married for more than 60 years, this was the last morning they would spend together in their home.

Olivia, ailing and feeble and too much of a burden to be adequately cared for by Charlie, was this morning being taken to live out her life in an assisted living facility.

. . .

Their time together had been what many would call charmed.

Married six days after Charlie returned home from the war in Korea, they owned and managed a neighborhood grocery store on the outskirts of Snohomish. They worked hard, and the business was good to them: they had twice expanded the size of the store as they became known and trusted for their fresh produce, home-cooked dishes and fair prices.

Over the years there had been three children (all still alive, one living in England), seven grandchildren and six great grandchildren. Along the way was a string of pets (Charlie had favored dogs and Olivia cats) and summer vacations enjoyed at their cottage in Anacortes on Fidalgo Island, usually with kids and then grandkids present.

Charlie had become quite an experienced fisherman, learning the art of studying Puget Sound and Pacific Ocean beaches at low tide to know exactly where the fish would be as the water surges toward high tide. He claimed it had something to do with "reading the pattern of broken seashells" strewn on the beach, and watching the sea birds.

As happens in all relationships, some rough times had occurred during the years, but always present was the abiding knowledge that their relationship was a most special and enduring one, and this infused the sharing attitude through which all challenges were met.

Twenty years ago they sold both their store and home and left Snohomish, retiring to the Anacortes cottage. Nestled on the outskirts of a protected fir and madrone forest, it brought them a much slower life. Their years there had been good ones: Olivia's wild flower garden was widely known and admired and Charlie constantly believed and referred to himself as the luckiest man in the North Pacific territories.

But age and decaying health had taken their toll, and life on their own together was no longer sustainable. Olivia's everyday needs required ongoing professional attention, and a local care facility had availability. So arrangements were made.

Reluctantly, sadly, today was the day Olivia was leaving their cottage home for good.

• • •

It had been a quiet morning, each woke early, lost in thoughts. Two small suitcases held all that Olivia was taking with her, they stood packed by the front door.

Outside, car doors close and after a few moments the doorbell rings . . . it is just before 10:00 am and the people from the facility are here for Olivia.

Charlie is going too, of course. He is planning to spend the day with her, returning home after dinner time. As he walked toward the door he paused to turn and look back into their home. On the ledge outside of the kitchen window a brown warbler ate from the pile of bread crumbs Olivia made sure was there each morning.

Thinking of the goodbye to come later that day . . . what could they say to each other? . . . what could he say to her? How desperately hard it will be to turn away, leaving Olivia, his life's partner, behind in the facility.

He follows Olivia and the attendants out.

Determined not to let Olivia see him cry, he pauses a moment, dabbing at his tears with his shirt sleeve, and then gently closes the door behind him.

• • •

Change -- often unwanted -- is the central feature of life. It can be both subtle and obvious; exhilarating, frightening, exhausting and relieving. It can spark sadness or happiness, resistance or grasping. It is always occurring, whether we seek it, try to hide from it or simply sit still and wait for it to find us.

Experiential insight into impermanence is central to Buddhist practice, as it points us toward equanimity in the midst of change and helps us to be wiser in how we respond to what comes and goes.

We often resist change. Trying to keep things the way they are, we cling to the supposed safety of permanence. But nothing actually stays the same for two consecutive moments -- whether a flash of lightning in the sky or a 60-year old loving relationship.

All is endlessly influx . . . moving toward and ultimately entering into inevitable stages of separation and cessation.

Everything is included. Every tree, every blade of grass, all the animals, insects, human beings, buildings, the animate and inanimate . . . everything is evolving, moment-by-moment.

Arising, coming together, maturing, aging, decaying and falling apart. Beginnings making endings possible and unavoidable.

Change. Always occurring . . . sometimes in hoped for, anticipated ways . . . and often not.

. . .

Charlies and Olivias exist everywhere.

Individual specifics might differ but we are all Charlie and we are all Olivia; caught up in the great dance, aware of movement, staring at impeding deadlines, seeing it all from our own side . . . hanging on and letting go, trying to make sense, unable to keep things as we want them to be . . . learning that nothing really belongs to us.

Occurrences all. Everything -- no matter how beautiful or seemingly mine or me -- gilded with impermanence . . . morphing and changing . . . becoming and unbecoming . . . the loop of burgeoning and swooning relationships within every single aspect of our lives.

Beware of those who traffic in reassurances of something other, or in ethereal fixes, no matter how eloquent or silver-tongued

-- there is no "solution" to the ongoing flow of impermanence. Rather, we acknowledge its ceaseless shelf-life and work with it as genuinely as we can.

From this work arises the realization that impermanence does not burden our life, but, quite to the contrary, animates it. Perhaps awakening to this is what we mean by the word "spiritual."

Siddhartha told us, "This existence of ours is as transient as autumn clouds. A lifetime is like a flash of lightning in the sky, rushing by, like a torrent of water down a steep mountain."

What to do?

Be aware and mindful, and then perhaps the great Persian poet Rumi's advice is best: "Come on sweetheart, let's adore one another before there is no more of you and me."

-- Am stopping my finger now, thank you for reading. (9.16.15)

Next Exit: Awakening!

I was traveling on the Interstate, driving from central Florida through Georgia and South Carolina into North Carolina. As many know, this is not our nation's most scenic route, but for billboard aficionados it is heavenly.

Big and attention-grabbing, they are lined up, one after another on each side of the road.

Besides advertising upcoming fast-food restaurants, motels and fueling stations, there are quite a few announcing what are called adult shops, in many cases trumpeting the added enticement of live girls.

Log the miles, read the signs.

Here's a sample (with make-believe name): "Visit Nasty Notions, your very own one-stop shop for sexy adult fun. Shop for birthdays, anniversaries, bachelor or bachelorette parties and special intimate moments. Huge inventory. We carry all adult products from lubes and lingerie to DVD's, from toys and extreme novelties to X-rated unmentionables."

While I haven't been tempted to stop in, I have been told that some of these shops are fronts for brothels. This may or may not be so, and while I suspect their sweet-spot targets are male drivers between the ages of 18-50, thousands of folks (including women and children) with no interest are forced to see these signs every day . . . they are billboards, they can't be turned off, deleted or avoided.

Discussing the yea's and nay's of these roadside attractions is for another time; seeing their signs hatched an idea I'd like to share with you.

• • •

Imagine a series of roadside Dharma shops strung along our highways, open 24/7, for people to stop and visit. Good for the entire family, offering a break from the grind of the road, the perfect stop for some nice tea (hot or ice) in an atmosphere of calm and safety.

They'll provide a sort of road-side mini-Disney experience, a refreshing Epcot-on-the-Highway . . . there to provide travelers with a respite of comfortable familiarity. Dharma-esque, 21st century Americana style. Softly lit, with sweet mantras piped out to the parking lot, Dharma tunes in the trees . . .

Upon entering, just inside, a rack of pithy t-shirts: "What Would Buddha Do?" and "Make Me One with Everything" and "Om Mani Padme Hum" (in authentic Tibetan lettering!) with images of Buddha-eyes or stupas or dorjes. Again, just t-shirts -- tourist fare, not too exotic . . . comfort zone stuff.

To suit individual needs, the shop will be organized into various experience-based sections . . . the 10th Bhumi Dharma-salon, the Corner of Wrathful Deities, and in the center All Things Buddha, complete with rear view mirror-hanging thangkas, images and statues (the smaller ones with sticky underneaths for convenient dashboard mounting).

Everything is displayed Tibetan-market style, with all items bar-coded for fast checkout, no time-consuming price haggling here. And, naturally, a kids' section, featuring -- for those seeking a touch of Disney -- a must-have headpiece complete with long Buddha ears and a dark blue Ushinisha atop, signifying resident wisdom. (Ordinary Mickey Mouse ears could never compete.)

There's no end to the possibilities. For a quarter kids can ride the mechanical Snow Lion (a Kodak moment?). Rest rooms renamed Yeti and Yeta, small "by-the-10-minute-chunk" meditation "caves" along the side wall (complete with Wi-Fi for those who find meditation boring), plastic Sword of Manjushri back-scratchers, and a multitude of Dalai Lama trinkets and authentic mass-produced self-knotting protection chords, imported from China to keep the production costs down and retailers' margins up.

Candles, yak-milk cheese, freeze-dried momos, teas, zafus and zabutons, yogs mats, bumper stickers and refrigerator magnets, little bags of Ganges sand and/or Himalayan rocks and various incense powder, cones and sticks will help round-out the Dharma-consuming experience.

And, of course, the best sellers: a line of specially made prayer flags, not with images of Tara or Medicine Buddha or the Windhorse but rather the logos of a favorite football team, reality TV star, NASCAR driver number, or, for a few extra dollars, a machine that'll take your or your kids' picture and imprint it on the flags, while you wait.

. . .

Along our Interstate highways we can buy triple-burgers and tacos, boutique phone cards and $49 overnight lodging, locally grown produce, rainbow slushies and discount cigarettes, fireworks, Americana handicrafts and "adult" products and experiences.

So why not some roadside enlightenment? Happiness sells, and it's a good alternative to the sex stuff -- it'll be cheaper, last longer, it's not as messy, can be shared with the kids and you can feel free to tell others about it without embarrassment.

And, imagine how your neighbors will covet the environment-friendly Buddha tote-bag your goods come in.

Share the vision, see the billboard now . . .

Next Exit: AWAKENING!

Be Who You Want to Be . . .

Bring some authentic Tibetan Buddhism home today . . .

Clean rest rooms! Easy on-and-off the highway!

-- Am stopping my finger now, thank you for reading.
(12.15.10)

It's a World of Teachers

Teachers.

People we learn from. They are everywhere, always have been.

They may be role models, guideposts, friends and/or sources of inspiration. They may also be creators of obstacles, hardship and disturbances.

Regardless of the form they take or the amount of time they spend in our lives, we frequently take them for granted, like or dislike them, accept or dismiss them, and then move on when they've gone. But the effects they've had on us, the lessons beyond the barriers to which they've led and then pushed us through, remain with us . . . stepping stones on the paths of our lives.

I write this having recently read of an ancient road that was uncovered during the construction of a subway in Thessaloniki,

Greece's second largest city. The marble-paved road was built by the Romans as the city's main artery of travel 2,000 years ago.

It got me thinking about some of the (now seemingly ancient) roads I've travelled in my 60+ years, and the people on those roads who have taught me my most significant lessons. Too numerous to mention more than just a small few here, some are:

> Johnny Look, who beat me up in a schoolyard fight I picked when I was about 15 years old. He taught me the important lesson of how easily I bleed when punched in the mouth (literally and figuratively).
>
> Mr. Irwin Wolfson, a junior high school English teacher whose passion for Shakespeare taught me not to be afraid to read writing I couldn't easily understand.
>
> Richard Brautigan, whose sweetly inventive (critics said 'childishly hippy') writings were my first exposure to what I now see were oddly spiritual sensibilities. Never had I read anyone with such wild imagination, poignant use of metaphor and off-beat under-statement. While I never got to meet him -- and have, following his suicide come to understand what a tortured being he was -- his ability to see and communicate unconventional perspectives has graced my thinking for years.
>
> Arnold Zeidel, who I met while hitch-hiking across the country in 1971 and who, while sitting around a late-night campfire at the Grand Canyon introduced me to Eastern thought by handing me a recently published book called *Be Here Now*.

Martin Fierro, a real-life Bodhisattva. Armed with a tenor saxophone and a truly sweet heart, Martin lovingly did his work in the guise of an Apache-born, clownishly irreverent musical genius.

People from various times in my life, completely different from one to another . . . and precious teachers, all.

• • •

We've all had teachers, even the greats were taught and influenced by others.

It's said that Hemmingway studied Turgenev, Thoreau loved Homer, Welty was inspired by Chekov. Faulkner claimed a debt to Joyce. Willie Mays idolized Jackie Robinson. Garcia was influenced by Joan Baez. Woody taught Arlo, as did Pete Seeger. Marcel Duchamp influenced Warhol. Trungpa taught Ginsberg. Oliver Wendell Holmes deeply influenced Felix Frankfurter, who then mentored Justice John Harlan. James Brown was said to have "taught" Michael Jackson how to dance.

The numbers and flavors of relationships between those who influence and those who are influenced are endless.

In the Buddhist systems, where teachers are identified and deeply appreciated, my eyes and ears have been opened widely by the teachings of Siddhartha Gautama, Thubten Yeshe, Shantideva, Dilgo Khyentse, Kalu Rinpoche, Dr. Alexander Berzin, Nagarjuna and Tsongkhapa, to name a few. And of course, humanity's current professor, His Holiness the 14th Dalai Lama of Tibet.

And there are many beings regarded as more "ordinary" both before and since I've been exposed to the fertility of the Buddhist teachings. I can now see them all as my teachers, presenting opportunities for me (sometimes forcibly, against my wishes) to learn and grow.

They've been of all ages, sizes, colors, faiths, political persuasions, sensibilities and inclinations. They include humans, animals, insects, etc. All teachers.

This perspective, the recognition of all these teachers, has taken me years to see and understand. It is endlessly rich and paves the way for true humility, appreciation and gratitude while keeping me open to absorb and learn from everyone whose path I cross.

. . .

This may be true for you too, so I leave you with a suggestion (if you're one who is inclined to be reading this I suspect it will not be a waste of time) . . .

Look at all the people in your life -- from years ago and those who are present now. Include those very close to you, and ones not so close: include friends and enemies, and those who are in between -- the neutrals.

Try to clear your mind of feelings of lingering attachment and/or aversion and ask yourself, with as honest and open a heart as you can: "What has this person taught me? How have they influenced me? What are they helping me to learn now? How have they, whether intentionally or not, created the conditions in which I was or am enabled -- or forced -- to grow?"

Allow what arises in your mind to do so without judgment . . . just the facts.

You will find that you've had -- and still have -- many teachers. And perhaps with new introspection you will, for the first time, see and appreciate them in a more significant and empowering way.

'Empowering' because it is quite possible this appreciation will lead to humility, and then to gratitude. And that gratitude will become a wish to settle any long-standing debts, to balance the ledger . . . to repay them for all they've led you to learn.

This payment won't be with money or material goods, but rather with the very thing their teachings have led you to: your best self . . . by becoming, with the best interests of others in mind, a more mindfully beneficial and well-meaning influence on all those whom you encounter.

In this way, you'll become an increasingly conscious teacher yourself. A role that, when honestly embodied, will be quite comfortable and feel immensely right.

And you will, therefore, do it very well.

-- Am stopping my finger now, thank you for reading.
(7.15.12)

The Hungry Self

Saturday dawned cool and foggy, a typical Pacific Northwest October morning, ideal for taking a drive into the mountains to poke around a bit.

We've been living in the Cascadian foothills for more than a year now, a time during which, unintentionally but inescapably, Kathy and I have been experiencing a deepening connection to the ecology of these northern mountains; countless old growth conifers, waterfalls and glacial creeks rushing into living rivers, knife-edged ridges cloaked in clouds and mist . . . all rustling through each other, unified weavings of an age-old tapestry.

Washington's northern Cascades are not the tallest mountains in the U.S. but they have dramatically sharp inclines and a thousand alpine lakes. From them I am reminded of Gary Snyder's words: "Range after range of mountains. Year after year after year. I am still in love."

Our usual path into the mountains is eastward through what is locally known as the Sky Valley, home to a string of towns and glens between Monroe and Skykomish and up to the Stevens

Pass. Through the rugged valley the Skykomish River travels westward, converging with the Snoqualmie River, the two becoming the Snohomish River which flows into Puget Sound at Port Gardner Bay.

The communities of the Sky Valley were founded in the mid-19th century by homesteaders whose livelihoods included logging, mining, farming and, beginning in the late 1890's, work connected with the Great Northern Railway.

Railway history in this region is romantic and rich. At one time eight passenger trains regularly ran into Seattle, stopping in Skykomish. These included some of the finest passenger trains in America -- the Great Northern Flyer, the Oriental Limited, the Cascadian, the Western Star and the Empire Builder. There was also a train affectionately known as the "Dinky" that went to Seattle in the morning and returned to Skykomish in the evening.

While freight transport remains active today, passenger service along the Great Northern's Sky Valley route ended in May 1971.

As one might expect, a number of old railway bridges and tunnels exist throughout the valley, some still active, others not. The active bridges are in good working shape, most of those no longer used are time-worn and rusty. But still they stand, stately in their survival; stubborn reminders of a not-so-long-ago era gone by.

. . .

Driving along an old logging road, Kathy and I approached an aging rail trestle stretched across a shallow river gorge, boldly grafitti'ed with a name (Arch) and a date. Bright yellow and clearly visible on the darkened metal, the writing was large and jarring.

It struck us as a trespass, a violation, visual litter. Kathy and I spoke of it for awhile. Seemingly much more than just a sign of modern times, it represented a moment of unthoughtful, immature behavior, a result of boredom or anger or a marking of turf... perhaps even done on a dare.

What Arch apparently intended to do was ensure that all who came here took notice of his name splayed across the bridge, becoming part of... no, actually now a focus of their experience there.

Did Arch consider this defacing to be an ugly interruption, a contamination he had no business or right to force upon others?

Maybe yes, maybe no. But that's of no matter... it's His idea, His name, His contamination, perhaps now, in his eyes, even His bridge. An act justified in a haze of self-cherishing, connecting him to this place and this place to him... likely "cool" in his eyes, an accomplishment, a source of pride.

Beneath the arrogance, why would anyone do this? What motivated Arch to think up and follow the idea, buy the paint, make the plans, sneak around, climb up on this scenic old bridge and then paint his name where he had no invitation to do so?

page 65

Would you do something similar? Engage in similarly aberrant behavior, intentionally foolish and destructive? So perverse and offensive ... clearly beyond the norm ... uniquely Arch, right?

Well, maybe it is unique to him in its intensity and personal style. But perhaps not in its motivating source.

Consider: this is little more than a graphically visual expression of the misunderstanding within which we all operate, in this case Arch's. It is confusion come to life, an over-the-top "notice me" act stemming from a yearning need that is common to most of us at various times.

It lives and hides deep in the heart of all human discontent, dissatisfaction, suffering and stress ... it is the often-exaggerated, always hungry -- and often starving -- delusion known as "our mistaken sense of self."

For most of us, a too-strong identification with ego (in Dharma studies, the ongoing self-centered fear that prevents us from cultivating impartial love, compassion and bodhicitta for all beings) feeds a pervasive attitude in our lives ... not just an idea but a persistent, mass culturally supported fever of "me."

Sometimes subtle, sometimes acute ... this fever is always lurking in the human mind.

It obscures the clear view of anything or anyone being equally or more important than ourselves. It is the source of all that ails us.

• • •

Here's the good news: while our self-orienting views are deeply held, like all else they are impermanent and subject to change.

So perhaps one day, usually unexpectedly, the quantum leap forward . . . something occurs, cracking the darkness, allowing us to know our "self" in a different, more realistic light . . . no longer being "the" light but simply one of many lights.

Perhaps this perception-changer is a dramatic one-time event: the death of a loved one, birth of a child, diagnosis of a frightening disease, etc. Or maybe it's something more ordinary: watching a sunset, seeing one's name among others in a telephone directory, or simply picking up a Dharma book and beginning to read.

This might arise anywhere, whatever the cause, the awakening effect is startling . . . a classical "aha" moment . . . when we first realize that the way we've always perceived the relationship between our self and others is rooted in a deep and ultimately harmful delusion.

And what's more, it's not only us who are afflicted. The delusion is immense: everyone is lost in it . . . with recurring confusion, discontent, stress, fear and suffering as a result.

Look around, see it for yourself.

This perceptual lack of "specialness of self" is an insightful realization. Buddhist teachings lead and then pass through it on the way to true peace, happiness and awakening. Intuitively reducing our sense of "it's all about me and mine" is a significant -- and necessary -- milestone along the Dharma path.

Vastly liberating, it is the quantum difference-maker.

Had our self-promoting friend Arch approached that railroad trestle with just a little bit of this awareness, some care for others, he might have been motivated to behave less selfishly, perhaps even more wisely ... for example, picking-up any trash he found lying around so that other visitors would have a purer view of the picturesque trestle.

Instead, self-invested by the ignorance that manifests as concern only for oneself, he arrogantly advertised himself for all to see.

• • •

Siddhartha taught that we perceive and experience the world around us through an easily exaggerated self-cherishing perspective; and he shared guidance on how we might create the conditions allowing that narrow perspective to evolve into one that is joyfully broad and beneficial.

It takes work; if you're on the Dharma path you know this to be true. Keep to it, remain diligent.

Dharma practice exposes self-imposed limits of unawakened thought and behavior. As you more clearly see the relationship between yourself and others from a wiser perspective (as you will), this will become increasingly difficult to ignore, and a great inner confidence will arise.

Allow it to emerge ... embrace it, breathe life into it and do what you know to be right. Let it become the framework of the sensibilities in which you exist.

Life is a constant serenade of change, and your shift from dwelling in self- to other-regarding inclinations will be among its most beautiful dances.

This shift will not be one you'll need to advertise, nor will it be one of selfish pride or ill-advised "Arch-like" activities.

Enriching to all whose path you cross, it will be the most profound "me" statement you can make . . . the fulfilling of your wisest, kindest potential.

-- Am stopping my finger now, thank you for reading. (10.21.15)

The Cape Canaveral Sutra

Thus have I heard.

Late that night the 21st Century Bodhisattva awoke in a small lagoon bordering the beach a short distance from where the rocket had thundered into space the day before.

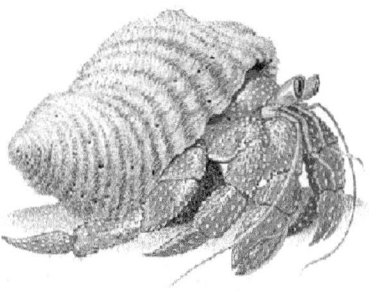

She found herself surrounded by shallow tide pools filled with innumerable sea creatures: crabs of various sizes and colors, starfish, urchins, snails and tiny fish; on the sand were turtles and frogs, alligators and snakes, small deer and otters and birds of every description . . . the wildness of the sea and the natural world it encompasses and supports.

All were still, watching curiously as she stretched and became aware of the myriad life gathered before her, sparkling in the brilliant glow of the full moon splintering through the trees overhead.

After several moments the Bodhisattva smiled; seeing this, a small crab approached and asked to hear a teaching that would illuminate the minds of all gathered there.

With a gentle gaze that encompassed all, she spoke softly: "No, it is you, not I, who needs to teach; it is you.

"It is your simple voices that are needed to awaken my self-centered human species . . . awaken us to the vast web of love and life and death we look beyond but of which you are aware each day. That to which your juices, fiber and chemistry are subject and make possible, as has been the case for so many centuries. I ask that you communicate to my species -- a species of blood, bone and muscle, confused in self-concept, arrogantly so -- speak to us in a language that is clear and unmistakable.

"Your voices are unfettered by the intellect my species has come to value so highly. Tell us of interconnection, of the life-giving elements you all share. Show us how to know that which so many have forgotten: the shared environment of all sentient being; the rhythms of the sun and moon, winds and clouds and storms, the brilliance of the nighttime sky, the deep and endless motions of the sea.

"In our complications, we humans have lost our connection to this, and wander from place to place, person to person, always looking for more or different, often in conflict with each other . . . day-to-day unaware of the web that you sustain . . . the web of which not only are we a part, but that we remain so dependent upon."

. . .

Gesturing toward the sky, the 21st Century Bodhisattva continued: "My species is capable of magnificence. From this very place we send ourselves to the stars in metal vessels, dependent on electronic intelligence machines and thunderous power, and yet we know not how to consciously enter the stream of genuine kindness, generosity, patience and love for each other. Sadly, it is a stream we seem to be afraid to enter yet which would provide such courage if we would only immerse ourselves in it.

"So, it is you, each of you, who should guide us . . . it is you who must teach, it is you who must show how we may all best survive and thrive on this planet. We need for you to do so . . . my species has lost the way."

"But we are simple creatures," said a krill who came forward, perplexed. "Many of us are seen as nothing more than food by your species. Teach? Instruct and guide humans? How can we do such a thing?"

As the Bodhisattva leaned closer, the sea creatures gathered around her more intimately. "When Siddhartha touched the Earth on that momentous evening, it was your ancestors, the beautiful, humble creatures of what we humans now call 'nature' -- as though it is something we are separate from -- that affirmed his achievement.

"At that time he was under the branches of the Bodhi tree, here tonight we sit beneath a similar canopy where we revisit and affirm the true interdependent nature of all sentient beings.

"Do not underestimate what you instinctively understand or

what you are capable of . . . it is clear to me, and will be to others as well. All beings carry the perfect understandings of buddha-nature in their mind, open to it, you will hear it speak to you. Recognize its voice and listen closely . . . it will guide you toward best achieving your aims."

All was still as the affirming words of the 21st Century Bodhisattva resonated within the minds of the assembled creatures of the sea.

She continued, "In your presence on this beautiful evening I am deeply humbled. On behalf of all members of my species, I bow before you and ask that you show us your knowing examples. We so very much need to learn from you . . . please."

After some time, in burgeoning determination the creatures of the sea disassembled and quietly set forth to fulfill the task with which they had been blessed.

-- Am stopping my finger now, thank you for reading.
(5.25.11)

Bo-dee-CHEE-ta

The Sanskrit word "bodhicitta" may be a foreign one, but let it roll off the tongue a few times and you'll notice its sweetness.

Upon saying it one tends to sing it ... bo-dee-CHEE-ta ... bo-dee-CHEE-ta ... it's hard to keep from smiling ... bo-dee-CHEE-ta ... can you feel that tasty little rise in energy on the CHEE? ... bo-dee-CHEE-ta.

What a wonderful set of conditions the term bodhicitta characterizes ...

The mind that is fully wise, fully compassionate.

The mind that is motivated to engage in Dharma studies and practices not simply to become stronger and more lovely (which it will), but is responding to the heart-felt knowledge that only with a mind that is calm and clear, kind and joyous, can one best help others overcome the confusion that is the cause of discontent.

By definition, Bodhicitta is the spontaneous wish to attain enlightenment, wholly motivated by great compassion for all sentient beings while propelled by a falling away of the attachment to the illusion of an inherently existing self, and the interconnections that become apparent as a result.

It begins with an attitude that is equally open towards all living beings, an equanimity that arises with the insight of shared natural potential. This is vastly different from attitudes arising from self-focused perspectives, which is how our own ego-grasping mind must see things in order to make its endless judgments.

Buddhist perspectives, practices and meditations bring understandings that, regardless of how others appear to my mind, they and I are deeply identical, beyond the mistakenly apparent layers of dualism and unique individuality.

All beings at the core are the same, simply wanting to experience happiness and avert suffering. It is upon this view that the initial foundations for bodhicitta are laid.

It's relatively easy for Westerners to intellectually understand the principles upon which Buddhist practices are based. Those who are intrigued by the Dharma can usually sense why Buddhist sensibilities and inclinations of intuitive loving-kindness and compassion are desirable, but as relative newcomers are initially perplexed about how to manifest and apply them.

The Mahayana path incorporates many contemplative methods that help bodhicitta blossom; one that is particularly useful is to build awareness of how much we depend on the kind and considerate actions of other beings.

Examine the variety of your needs and the richness of your pleasures. Include everything you enjoy in life, everything you use or need. Account for every single thing, and things in all combinations ... all the people, every bit of food and drink, all your clothes, your entertainments, love and affection, communications, travels, transportation, events, happenings,

medicines, employment, whatever you can think of, whatever you can point to and say "this" or "that."

Exclude nothing.

If you take the time to quiet down and consider how all of it comes to be, including yourself, you'll find that every bit is -- and always has been – dependent upon and made possible by others ... many, many others, and only an infinitesimal number of these beings are ones you've met or know anything about.

Spread far and wide, they are nothing more than nameless strangers, anonymous people of no importance, apparently deserving none of your consideration or caring.

Even though they have a profound effect on virtually every aspect of your and your loved ones' lives ... you go on, day after day with nary a thought of gratitude or appreciation ... if you think of them at all.

We trust they'll always be there, these nameless, faceless people, our infinite support system, doing what they do, providing what they will, all for our benefit. We do so with nary a thought of gratitude or appreciation.

Such are the ways of self-centeredness. Such are the ways of the narrow mind prisons we create for ourselves ... and live within.

• • •

But then one day we stumble upon the Buddhist teachings and perspectives. Drawn in, we begin to see it all, how the system works ... there's so much ... great kindness, universal dependency, all beings interconnected.

To see it as it is, clearly, for the first time is awakening, transformative ... humanizing. It's so plain and clear to see, how could it have remained unknown for so long?

Bo-dee-CHEE-ta ... Bo-dee-CHEE-ta ...

• • •

Each time we eat we pay no mind to the efforts of so many people that make our food possible, nor the pain and destruction of so many creatures; their homes and the places they've lived being destroyed ... plowed under, farmed ... all so that we may eat.

If we eat meat, or chicken, or fish ... what about taking those bodies for our own nourishment and enjoyment? These beings who provide their bodies for us to enjoy and grow strong from.

Think about it. Take some time, clear your mind, reflect. There is nothing we have, nothing we are that doesn't come to us through the efforts -- and often the sacrifices -- of others.

Can you see the undeniable truth in this? How very clear it all is? If so, where does it take you? How does it make you feel?

If this is of interest to you, if it resonates, take an honest look at how you exist and all the support -- direct and/or indirect -- every being provides for you.

Consider that if not for countless others, your life would not have happened, you could not possibly be here now to love and travel, to have children and learn and be the presence you are for your friends, family and community.

If you can stay on this -- and certainly not everyone is willing to try -- you may begin to feel the stirrings of precious bodhicitta.

Its source is not mysterious -- it arises from the gratitude born of awareness of the never-ending everything web all beings, including you and I, share in.

Bo-dee-CHEE-ta . . . Bo-dee-CHEE-ta . . .

Bodhicitta. It is a Sanskrit word . . . it may be new to you, but it defines something very ancient and profound . . . it is the name of your deepest precious human potential.

When arising it is unmistakable. Well-being abounds, as does a deep confidence, and you intuitively understand why you have the sense the whole world is taking care of you, making each moment of your life possible . . .

Because it is.

-- Am stopping my finger now, thank you for reading.
(5.29.13)

She Arises . . .

She keeps coming, arising. Manifesting as beneficial emanations from deep inside, say those who know . . . her vision clear, her voice confident and strong.

She is your wisest self -- your very best mind, your kindest heart.

She is in each and every step you take.

She abides in the pockets of your clothes, between the toes on your feet and the lashes of your eyes.

She comes in moments of love, as well as in moments of love going wrong.

She is there when sleep won't come because your mind cannot quiet down, and you spend the night gazing up at the ceiling.

She floats through the melodies of your lullabies, in your worlds of dreams and nightmares and in the reliving of memories.

She is there as you hold loved ones in your arms, and remains after you let them go.

She moves you toward moments of freedom and imagination, helping to free you when you are confused and distracted.

She shared in your first breath, and will be with you at the time of your final one.

She never stops coming.

She is there when you pray and she is there when you curse. She is patient, always waiting for you to come back to her through your angers and lusts, disappointments and excitements.

Her ideas are presented through the lineage teachings of Manjushri and Maitreya, Chenrezig and Shantideva, Tsongkhapa, Tenzin Gyatso and countless bodhisattvas who live in -- and ignite in others -- true wisdom and compassion.

In today's world of icons and symbols, as a man her image is among the most recognizable ... the Buddha ... but unlike representations of outer things, this vision is simply a projection of you, and all you can be.

Her essence lives in the minds of all sea and air creatures and those who live on the land. All creatures, whether youthful or elderly ... healthy or ill ... vibrant or dying ... asleep or awake.

In whatever country or neighborhood, city or forest, canyon or shoreline . . . in midday sunlight or midnight darkness, Sunday or Monday or any other time, she is there with you.

She is indescribable wakefulness for those who have gathered the accumulations in support of her coming, and have purified the obscurations that have in the past blocked her way to you.

She arises with profound presence in the mind that understands and remains mindful of the latent influences of karma, and seeks to cultivate merit for the benefit of others.

She intensifies as confusion dawns into understanding.

She arises in minds that know nothing can be created or exist independently of its parts, nor can anything be destroyed into nothingness.

She arises in the minds of all who take full responsibility for their perspectives, motivations, intentions and actions.

She comes to those who remain aware of the profound difference between how mind seems to be, and how mind really is.

. . .

Her path is known as Dharma.

Her reason for being is to help eliminate the causes of stress, discontent, suffering.

She is safety.

She is brilliance.

She is fearlessness.

She is happiness born of well-being.

She is selfless compassion.

She is the most virtuous you can be at each and every moment.

She provides guidance when you engage in anything that matters ... and gently reminds you that everything matters.

In her final human rebirth she manifested as a male -- a prince -- but in mind is neither solely male or female. Embracing both, she manifests beyond the limitations of each.

In that human life her name was Siddhartha Gautama. As a man she awakened and became the great professor, known to all for centuries to come as the Buddha.

The perfection she uncovered in her mind exists in yours as well. Your unrealized capabilities are equally as empowering, just as perfect as hers, regardless of the spiritual or religious path, if any, you follow.

Study, contemplate, meditate, uncover ... engage.

She is the Tathagata, the one "gone beyond."

She is your best mind.

She keeps coming, arising dependently ... and bearings of her arisings are, as they always have been, dependent solely upon you.

-- Am stopping my finger now, thank you for reading.
(4.19.15)

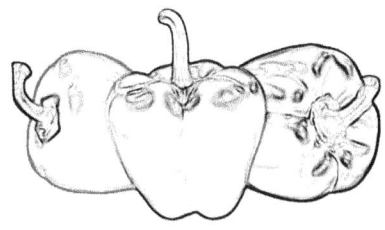

Crutches and Bell Peppers

If you're in Quebec City and drive north along the western shore of the St. Lawrence River, after an hour you'll come to the Basilica of Sainte-Anne de Beaupré.

The chapel was built by early French Jesuit settlers in 1658 to house what was believed to be a miraculous statue of Sainte Anne.

By 1688 it had become a site of local pilgrimage, and by 1707 Huron native Americans (who in Canada are called the First Nations) were coming to venerate the Sainte they called "Grandmother in the Faith."

The first miraculous healing attributed to the intervention of Ste. Anne at Beaupré was the curing of a crippled workman in

1658. This was followed by the unexplained and very unlikely safe deliverance of a group of sailors from a deadly storm in 1670.

Miracles and spontaneous healings continued to be associated with the miraculous statue, some believe in concert with the healing waters that flow in the ground beneath the church. These phenomenal purifications have continued over the centuries to the present day.

A chapel in the basilica is stacked with crutches, canes, body braces, collars, shoes, supports and wheelchairs no longer needed, accessories left behind by those who arrived infirm but, having been healed of their afflictions, were able to walk from the basilica without them.

At all times, a battery of votive candles flicker in the chapel's dim light, said to be "burning witnesses" of the ardent faith of those pilgrims who come to be freed of their afflictions.

I have visited the Basilica of Sainte-Anne de Beaupré more than once, not as a pilgrim but as one of the many tourists who come from around the world to simply be there. It is extraordinary . . . energetically bountiful and fiercely empowering, rendering insignificant any disuniting particularities of one's religious beliefs or practices.

The idea of a sacred place, spiritually fertile, where one with faith and immersed in the resident "zest" can overcome crippling afflictions, has always captured my imagination . . . and, as metaphor, reinforced my motivational Buddhist fancies.

Hence the following . . .

• • •

There's a place in Washington's eastern Cascades, in the heart of what's known as the Alpine Lakes Wilderness that Eleanor and John like to visit. It is locally known as the Enchantments, a wonderland of soft tundra meadows, glacial lakes, crystal clear streams and impossibly massive granite rock formations.

After a not-too-long hike from one of the trail-heads, one enters a beautiful low-grass alpine meadow, complete with a flowing stream leading to a waterfall at the meadow's far end.

When Eleanor and John visit, they like to bring along several fresh organic bell peppers of different colors -- green, red, yellow and orange, as well as some (deep blue) lapis lazuli stones that John brought back from the Himalayas in years past.

They have a favorite afternoon-sunlit place in the meadow, a flat spot near the waterfall, on which they spread a treasured blanket of Eleanor's. On the blanket, which is used only on their visits to the Enchantments, they place some votive candles, a small Chenrezig statue and two sandalwood malas. Just beyond the edge of the blanket they dig a small hole in the ground, and sit together facing it.

They settle into the environment and after some quiet moments begin to grind the lapis into a gritty powder, and cut the peppers into pieces.

Softly spoken intentions of morality, prayers and six-syllable mantra recitations follow, and then in turn each selects a piece of pepper to which a recently experienced klesha (unwholesome, afflictive emotion) is attributed, imputing that emotion onto/into the pepper slice. (Red seems to be the color they most commonly identify kleshas with.)

Then a pinch of lapis powder is sprinkled on the pepper piece, signifying the presence of the curative strength and purity of the Medicine Buddha. The assigned klesha emotion is softly communicated to the other and then the pepper, now an offering, is gently laid in the hole.

With each offering, Eleanor and John visualize they are helping purify the karmas and delusions of the sentient beings of the six realms, clearing the way for bodhicitta to arise in their minds.

This is done with each piece, one after another.

They take their time with this . . . understanding the causes for these afflictive emotions, deeply seated in sentient minds, are not so easily dislodged.

• • •

Their practice is both solemn and joyous, at times each intensely so.

Sometimes John and Eleanor pause and simply hold hands, content to be just an aspect of it all. They talk about the Dharma, the precious teachings that nourish so many. They reflect upon those in their lives they know and care for, both human and animal. They share how fortunate they are to have found each other. They also laugh alot.

More peppers go into the klesha hole . . . one after another .
. . each representing and removing a mental state that arises
to cloud the mind and manifest in unwholesome action --
anger and grasping, frustration and arrogance, fear and greed,
insecurity and envy, anxiety, depression, hatred, conceit, delusion,
confusion, doubt, torpor, restlessness, craving and clinging . . .
and the mother of all kleshas -- the self-cherishing thought, the
direct progeny of ignorance.

. . .

The atmosphere is spectacular, to be in the midst of such natural
beauty overwhelms . . . so invigorating, so wholesome.

With each visit this alpine meadow is becoming, more and
more, a familiar wilderness home to John and Eleanor. They
are grateful to have found it, this natural lea that is everything
they want it to be . . . a shared place of cleansing, of removing
obstacles and limitations, of freedom, of healing . . . a place of
release from all boundaries . . . a garden of bodhicitta.

After some time they fill in the hole, gather their belongings
and head back to the car, often softly singing. With minds
more open and less hindered by kleshas, their walk out differs
from the walk in. The ground now seems a bit softer, their steps
lighter, the wilderness colors richer, the sounds of birds heard
as the enchantingly sweet ting-ting of Hum . . . perfect little
bodhicitta bells.

In each of their minds is an ardent faith, a familiar knowing . .
. assenting a deep sense of inspired, open-minded welcome . . .
an unshakable understanding that whatever is to come will be

experienced as opportunities for virtue ... Dharma moments ... met and embraced with increasing clarity and ease.

Good hearts. Fertile minds ... purified and clear ... confident, hopeful ... increasingly capable.

And, as Eleanor loves to humorously remind John, everything -- including their minds -- completely empty of it all.

. . .

Years and distance melt together, as do virtuous paths of belief and practice.

It's not difficult to see Eleanor and John's feelings and thoughts, nurtured by Tibetan Buddhist sensibilities, as close kin to those of deep faith who, through the years, left their crutches and braces behind in that glorious French Canadian cathedral ... at long last walking freely and unencumbered into the rest of their lives.

-- Am stopping my finger now, thank you for reading.
(1.14.15)

A Hint of Tibetan Juniper

Dhih (pronounced deee) is the seed syllable of perfect wisdom (prajnaparamita). It derives from the old Vedic root dhī, incorporating a range of meanings including: to perceive, think, meditate, or reflect; understanding, intelligence, knowledge and wisdom.

In practice it is associated with Manjushri, the bodhisattva representing wisdom (or, as some say, the Buddhas' genius). It sits at the end of the mantra of Manjushri: OM A RA PA TSA NA DHIH.

In the mantra the individual syllables preceding Dhih have no conceptual meaning but are seen as symbolic connectors with various vibrational/spiritual qualities. Chanting the Manjushri mantra is said to enable arising wisdom and improve one's skills in debating, memory, writing, explaining, etc. When chanting the mantra, the DHIH is pronounced with greater emphasis then the preceding syllables.

• • •

Himachal Pradesh, India. As is usual for this time of year (December), the skies were clear and temperatures low; the Himalayan peaks snow-covered in the northern distance.

The Bir Tibetan Colony, in the foothills of the great mountains.

It was late afternoon, there were not many people out and about, but small groups of men huddled in front of the various storefronts that lined Bir's unpaved main road.

It had been a long, rugged drive from Dharamsala, and the American was stiff as he emerged from the car. The town appeared as had been described: picturesque but rubbish-strewn, tea plantations on the hillsides; a Tibetan refuge colony much as one might visualize pre-tourist-onslaught Dharamsala was 30 years ago, before becoming an international must-visit destination. Nothing fancy, but genuine.

The American would be in Bir for a few days, coming down to warmer climes from the winter cold of the McLeod Ganj ridgetops. He had been there for the past few months, learning to speak Tibetan, working on his Buddhist meditation practice and sharing conversational English with Tibetan refugees.

Chokling Monastery was to be his place of lodging in Bir. Being the highest structure in town it was easy to spot in the distance and he made his way toward it.

Upon arriving all was unexpectedly quiet, no one seemed to be around.

The Chokling complex is a large one, comprising buildings, stupas and gardens. He entered the main courtyard, walked toward the largest building and tried a couple of doors before finding one unlocked.

Once inside he was in the gompa, the prayer hall. A large room, it was empty and cold, gloomy almost, dim in the lowering daylight. There were a few butter lamps burning on a table and a faint earthy aroma of Tibetan incense.

Weary from his travels and grateful to have finally arrived, the American had the notion to "acclimate" to Bir by sitting in meditation for a time before seeking anyone out.

He approached and sat before the grand Shakyamuni Buddha statue on the altar. It was raw-chilly in the empty gompa, and he wrapped himself in a wool shawl he pulled from his backpack.

As in many of the far-from-home Himalayan Buddhist sites he had visited, once settled, the sitting was easy. Immersed in a distinctively peaceful and emerging "this also is my home" atmosphere, before long the American's mind was resting calmly in single-point concentration.

• • •

After some time he sensed a gentle swish of warm air accompanied by the woody scent of juniper, and he became aware of a presence sitting before him. Gently opening his eyes he saw it was an elderly man, Tibetan, in the robes of a lama. Although the American could not recall ever seeing this lama before, he seemed familiar. Smiling softly, the American continued in his meditation.

After a few minutes he heard the lama speak, "say with me . . . dhih . . . dhih . . . dhih . . . gently, just for me to hear . . . dhih . . . dhih . . . dhih . . . not too quickly, in flow on the breath, one to the next . . . dhih . . . dhih . . . dhih . . ."

The American did so, in a whisper . . . dhih . . . dhih . . . dhih . . . As an effortless momentum began to blossom, he continued with deepening surety . . . dhih . . . dhih . . . dhih . . . dhih . . . dhih . . .

He again heard the lama's voice, closer, seemingly inside his own mind, as he continued "dhih. . . dhih . . ." It guided him to place his hands out at his sides, and as he did he sensed a motion similar to spinning in a circle, in place. With the movement, the dhih . . . dhih emerged more rapidly from both his mind and his lips, rhythmically synchronized with his body's swirling.

Never had he experienced anything like this, but he knew he was safe; there was no danger, no need to hold back or grasp for control.

The dhih . . . dhih . . . dhih . . . was now coming as rapidly as he was capable of producing the sound . . . dhih . . . dhih . . . dhih . . . dhih . . dhih . . dhih . . dhih . dhih . dhih . dhih dhih dhih dhih didhdidhdidhdidhdidhdidh . . . and then vocalization became impossible as the lama had become a moist warm cloud, a mist, entering his mouth, filling it as it spread into his head and throat and down through his chest . . . absorbing into his breath, penetrating and filling his organs and nervous system, soaking into every cell of his body.

• • •

After some time the American's movement slowed and gradually came to a stop. There was no aftermath of dizziness or imbalance, just a deep peace.

He was no longer saying dhih . . . dhih, there was no need.

He had become dhih, he was nothing but dhih.

Dhih was everything: his breath, his mind. Flashes of perfect understanding were bursting inside every sensation and thought . . . dhih was all he was, all he could be . . . it was his entire experience.

He sat in that way for a long while; unmoving, his eyes resting closed. Everything about him was soft; his ear consciousness purring, his eye consciousness immersed in pastel.

And his being . . . limitless, endless . . . completely knowing. Transcendence dawning, an awareness of all . . . indescribable . . . his mind an infinitely-faceted, perfectly flawless jewel . . . bottomless . . . brilliantly clear.

When the moment seemed right he slowly opened his eyes.

Time and place seeped into his consciousness. He was in the same spot, wrapped in his shawl . . . he hadn't moved. There was no lama, only the Buddha was before him. Besides the gompa having grown darker, everything was as it had been when he first sat down.

But for him nothing was as it had been before.

・・・

It had started out as a short sit ... a rest ... just a meditative "hello" to a few days in Bir, but it had become so much more.

A small, knowing nod to the Buddha, and then, with eyes moistened by gratitude, prostrations of respect to the lama ... to all lamas, everywhere. He packed his shawl away and turned to leave.

As he did, he noticed for the first time the Manjushri thangka hanging from the ceiling high above his head. It seemed to be swaying as if in a slight breeze, but he could feel no breeze; all was completely still.

Then, a hint of Tibetan juniper ...

-- Am stopping my finger now, thank you for reading.
(4.0.12)

Semesters' End

It is a high school classroom like any other, a large room in an ordinary one-story cinder block building, but it's a room that for more than 20 years had been alive with the energy of a very special history teacher.

The Teacher is a friend who was forced to abruptly stop and retire from a lifetime of teaching a few months ago upon receiving a serious medical diagnosis. He is now in treatment, doing well, but the retirement stands. I met him and his roommate early one morning to help empty out his classroom.

I have worked in a number of organizations and observed the work habits of many people, but I have never known anyone more dedicated to his work (i.e., his students) than the Teacher, now in his classroom for the final time.

Into boxes went hundreds of carefully compiled binders, full of laminated pages that over the years had helped teach students about black history, women's rights, the American Constitution and Bill of Rights, ancient and current world events, warriors and peace creators, Nobel Prize winners and global criminals.

Files on Thomas Jefferson and Malcolm X, Dr. Martin Luther King, Jr. and Benjamin Franklin, Margaret Sanger and Thurgood Marshall among others were packed away.

There were piles of local news clippings; many had become stale and dusty as in recent years Florida's state-mandated focus on institutional testing had removed the ability to stray from the approved high school curriculum of study. So there was no longer time for what the Teacher referred to as "the fabric" -- the relevant issues and people behind the events that he knew to be critical for his students' most meaningful understandings.

The underlying message within all he taught was a simple one: as has always been, every day provides opportunities for accomplishment and growth. He taught history from the perspective of it being made not by special beings but rather by ordinary people thrust into situations where they could be special, and took the steps to be so.

In other words, noteworthy impact being made by people no different than any of the students he was teaching.

This is a teacher who was most interested in seeing his students develop into decent human beings, and he saw the unlimited potential for broad-minded accomplishment in each student who sat before him.

Given his druthers, he would have wanted -- and worked tirelessly toward -- his students' report cards looking something like this:

-- Writing Letters to Those You Love: **A+**

-- Investigating and Appreciating the Critters who Live in Your Backyard: **A+**

-- Developing the Confidence to Follow Your Wise Heart: **A+**

-- Experiencing History as a Chain of Events of Which You Are a Part: **A+**

-- Putting Others Before Self: **A+**

-- Taking Responsibility for Each Aspect of Your Own Life: **A+**

-- Being Honest: **A+**

-- Respecting Those Who Came Before You, and Accepting Responsibility for Those Who Will Come After: **A+**

. . .

The Teacher is by nature a proud, self-professed "diligent" pack-rat; there must have been close to 100 boxes taken from his classroom and loaded into the borrowed truck.

Boxes containing years of teaching, each with innumerable memories of faces and exchanges with students, challenges and accomplishments ... the husks of countless seeds planted in fertile minds that grew to love, trust and appreciate him as each semester progressed.

I know the Teacher plans to donate much of this material to local history groups and libraries, but he is not sure if they will want it.

This makes me wonder . . . how many of us have piles of boxes of personal stuff in our closet or attic or basement, holding contents forgotten yet too treasured to throw away, being held onto as if someday we'll actually have the time and inclination to go through and re-experience them? Or if others will care about them as we do?

. . .

Once the truck was packed we went back to ensure nothing had been left behind. The room was different now; it was empty, strikingly barren, all traces of warmth and comfort had been removed. After a quick look around the roommate and I went out into the hall, leaving the Teacher alone in his classroom to say goodbye.

A few moments later the lights went out and the Teacher emerged, shutting the door gently behind him.

He looked at us, smiling through his sadness, this man who was born to teach and would do so no longer.

Softly, he said just one word, "Impermanence," and then slowly walked away from what for him had been so much, but was now nothing more than what used to be.

-- Am stopping my finger now, thank you for reading. (6.22.11)

A $10 Million Question

Sharing in the Dharma for some years now, we've had our challenging moments.

Florida's Lake County is not an area with Buddhism on every street corner, and some come to the Dharma very much rooted in their own ideas and beliefs, unwilling to do much more than listen and see how the Buddha's teachings might prop up their own deeply held notions.

Some students understand how to cultivate awareness/mindfulness and ways to practice but don't really bother; others don't know how, nor do they care to find out. And then there are those who come to the Dharma curious but full of doubt... instinctively skeptical, as if allowing their mind to open and explore new perspectives is something to fear and distrust.

Everyone wants to be happier, experience less suffering and be well-thought of and loved, but so many seem truly disinterested (afraid?) in opening to and walking the path that leads to identifying and overcoming the obstacles that prevent those things from manifesting.

• • •

We recently held a retreat in Gainesville (FL) during which we engaged in an assortment of activities, from calm-abiding meditations to practice visualizations and chanting (Chenrezig and Vajrasattva mantras). All our activities were done in union with a shared reading of Padampa Sangye's 12th century *One Hundred Verses of Advice*.

As we worked our way through these pithy verses, which were composed and delivered by Padampa to his "People of Tingri," we were repeatedly reminded of the magnificent preciousness of human life, the beyond-imagination capabilities of our minds and the virtuous wholesomeness of the Mahayana path.

Sometimes when we read or hear something, especially during teachings when so much is being discussed, we let it rest on our mind for a few moments, without the opportunity to truly reflect upon it.

Not to allow our Dharma appreciation(s) to slip by without due consideration, I posed a question to each person in attendance: If you could receive $10 million to forget all the Dharma you've ever learned and experienced ... all your insights about karma and impermanence, emptiness and compassion ... all of it, every bit, and by so doing slip back into the mind (including the perspectives, lack of self-knowledge, insights, friendships, etc.) you had before first encountering the Dharma, would you do it?

(And I ask you, dear reader to consider ... would you?)

...

Very few if any of our students are independently wealthy, everyone has worked for living, many are retired and on fixed income ... needless to say, $10 million is a lot of money; it would buy many things, enable much, solve many hardships and problems.

So there it is: instant wealth simply by walking away with no Dharma recollections, no recall, no Dharma understandings or insights or remembered experiences ... no familiarity.

Pretty dramatic ... $10 million in hard cash right at the moment, here and now ... to forget the Buddha, Dharma and Sangha ... to leave it all behind, have no trace left in the mind, no memory of its existence.

There were smiles on thoughtful faces, and then in their own way each and every person shook their heads no, they would not revert to the unknowing, the unawareness. Their enriched minds, adorned by travels and experiences on and of the Path are too precious, too valuable, too dear -- not for sale, even for $10 million ... or by inference, any price.

One after another, no deal.

As we let that sit for a while, an ambiance of satisfied

appreciation spread. Then I asked the hard question.

If each of us considers our mind to be so precious, if our acquired Dharma richness is more dear to us than instant wealth, why do we not practice with more diligence?

Why do we engage in the self-cherishing intentions and behaviors -- not intentionally evil or harmful, of course -- that set the mind back, defile and complicate it, creating obstructive karmic seeds and occurrences?

Why do we infuse our minds with hours of manipulative, agitating television each night, and not treat those in our life with the deepening patience, generosity, love and joyful enthusiasm our health-seeking mind yearns to manifest, and is increasingly ready to give rise to?

Why do we continue to so instinctively consider ourselves to be more special, more deserving and more important than others?

Why do we waste so much time, allowing fertile Dharma opportunities to pass by as meaningless, unfulfilled moments?

If experiencing the wisdom and compassion of our mind is so valuable to us -- $10 million worth -- why are we so lazy, doing things that, as Dharma students, we're acutely aware create harm and difficulty, that contaminate and pollute our evolving minds, and obstruct our manifesting the enhanced states and qualities of being we value so highly?

When it comes to study and/or practice, many of us use the excuse "there's no time!" . . . our days are so busy, there's so many things, so much work to do . . . simply no time to formally dedicate to Dharma, my "self" is simply too busy.

As if Dharma is something we do only when time permits, when there's nothing else going on.

. . .

Considering the high value many people put on "Dharmatizing" their lives in relation to the conscious effort made to actually achieve it, there is a clear disconnect here.

Perhaps for some, the Dharma mind is really just another aspect of self-centeredness . . . a high-regarding aspect of "me" . . . a self-identity that I treasure and don't want to lose because I like how it makes me feel. (If this resonates for you, don't fret.

This is quite normal for those in the beginning phases of their Dharma experiences, and may manifest for years . . . be honest, see it and work with it.)

Or perhaps you see your mind's emerging beauty, clarity and strength as tools not just for your own benefit but for that of others . . .

Please check-up and see where you come out on this.

. . .

Consider:

Practicing Dharma is just like breathing. While working, we breathe, while sleeping we breathe, while sitting down and eating and making love, we breathe.

We have time to breathe due to the necessity and importance of our breath ... and really have no real choice not to.

In the same way, considering the profound importance and preciousness of our mind, and the vastly beneficial impact Dharma practice has on every aspect of our life, perhaps we will find the will and the time to practice and engage accordingly.

Our practice provides experience that infuses our mind with boundless wealth. The Buddha didn't praise those who merely acquired material objects or the opinions of others, he praised those who endeavored to know within themselves.

Spend some time, investigate this ...

I believe it's likely that if forced to choose between the two -- Dharma Wealth vs. Extreme Material Wealth, even at $10 million -- the depth of cultivating and abiding in the enlightening mind will win out.

It's a wonderful exercise. Dig into it and, once done (and depending on which direction your karma propels you), follow your intuitive voice.

-- Am stopping my finger now, thank you for reading.
(6.7.12)

Fridge Samsara

I was up early for my thrice-weekly sunrise walk along the lake shore with my friend Guenter. The kitchen was dark and as I filled the teapot with water, I thought I heard voices coming from the refrigerator.

As I tip-toed closer it was unmistakable, there was talking coming from inside the box. I sat down, put my ear against the door and listened. The voices were easily identifiable although I could not see them being spoken.

"Yipeeee, here we go, another day," said the bottle of apple juice.

"Easy for you to say," said the milk. "You stay nice and fresh in this cold, but as I mature I'm destined to turn lumpy and sour. Soon I'll be nothing but cheese. My days here are numbered."

Hearing this, the Gouda perked up. "Well, milk, that's tough luck, but don't knock being cheese. If you had gone through the hard work of being made into the right kind of cheese, you wouldn't have to worry about going sour. My milk was grass-fed . . . my pedigree is top-shelf!"

"Well, excuse me, Chunk-o-Cheese, what do you have to be so proud about? . . . you're nothing but a slab of controlled dairy decay," said a red delicious apple, "and besides, compared to me you're so mushy soft and such a blasé color . . . you only wish you could be crisp and red and beautiful like me."

"Ha," said the tuna salad to the apple. "You're so proud because you have a nice color, but you spent your entire life hanging from just one branch on a tree no different from those around it. Me, I am a majestic fish. I swam the ocean, free and wild, and saw everything there was to see."

"Ah, but look at you now," said the egg, "you were a ruffian, once toothy and scaly . . . now you're all chopped up, held together by a scoop of mayonnaise, which couldn't be made without me. I am indispensable . . . see me as I am . . . the sensitive, gracefully curved, always-handled-gently-by-the-human egg."

"Oh, you're all such simple creatures; nothing special, nothing mysterious," drawled a can of Coca Cola. "Now me, I'm complex. My secret ingredients are kept in a super-security safe in headquarters in Atlanta, and my home is this beautiful metal cylinder designed by the greatest marketers in the land. We all know the human reaches for me first when he opens the door on a hot day. And you only wish you had a pop-top like mine. Indeed, things go better with me."

"Yeah, and the human always burps after he drinks you, brown fizzy" quipped the bottled spring water. "But me, I go down smooth, am completely refreshing, and there's nothing in my DNA that will rot his teeth."

"Flat and unexciting," muttered the seltzer. "Smooth water is for bathtubs. No bubbles is boring."

On the lower shelf, the organic yogurt looked over at the Dijon mustard and smugly whispered, "listen to that rabble up there, they all think they're so great. But down here, in the quieter place, it is best. Only those of us who are special can be on this shelf. Just the thought of this makes my cultures bubble with pride."

"Mais oui, mon chere," said the mustard. "Such losers up there, so special we are. But, my curdy friend, while you're natural, you're just a cup of bacteria. Me, I'm so precious that the human only uses a very little bit of me at a time . . . to his taste buds I am a delicacy."

"Yes, you're a delicacy, Frenchie, but your continental cultural roots are far away. My cultures are alive, and I'm healthy for the human. I am probiotic, you probably don't even know what that means. You merely taste good, but are otherwise useless."

"Useless? Sacre bleu, tres arrogant . . . how dare you think that?" the Dijon stammered, his lid spinning . . .

It was at this point that Diogi barked at something outside, and all became silent inside the refrigerator.

page 111

So there it was. Self-centeredness ... arrogance ... the superiority of me, myself and I. Samsara exists everywhere, even in the cool recesses of the kitchen.

Gently, I opened the fridge door and took out a red delicious apple and yogurt. Mindfully aware they could hear me, I thanked them for their nourishment as I sat down to breakfast.

-- Am stopping my finger now, thank you for reading. (7.7.10)

"Mani Brings Money"

February 20, 2013

From: Charles Cavallo, CEO

Memo to: All Sales Employees

Hello Noble Ones:

As many of you remember, we enjoyed a different type of motivational speaker (Fred "Call Me Lama" Cheetem) at our annual sales meeting last month.

Besides being entertaining and inspiring, Lama Cheetem has devised a custom curriculum for us in which updated aspects of ancient Buddhist teachings may be adapted and executed to achieve greater corporate bottom-line health.

While it is true that the Buddha is believed to have lived centuries ago in a culture very unlike our own, many of his notions that Cheetem-la shared with us -- remember, they were called "Dharma" -- are about to become building blocks for our rejuvenated sales policies and methodologies.

We are updating our Employee Handbook to reflect many of these exciting new ideas. In advance of its publication I'd like to review Three Principal Aspects of our new sales outreach program with you here and now:

   1. **Awareness and mindfulness** are the bastions of beneficial presentation, negotiation and client relationships. During working hours constant and persistent awareness should be paid to "what can I be doing to best benefit the company?" regardless of where you are, what you are doing and who you are doing it with. Mindful awareness that every sale (or customer) lost will result in less income for the company -- and perhaps the loss of your job -- must be maintained.

<u>Note</u>: To help you with this, our Training group is developing a "True Happiness Arises Once the Client Pays" meditation program (our blessing mantra to be Om Ah Ka-ching Hum ... the folks in legal are securing the trademark). More details soon.

   2. **Generosity.** The Buddhist teachings apparently say that those who are experiencing generosity are most happy. Please work to establish this truism in your clients; be passionate and skillful in generating generosity in their minds as you are engaged in negotiations leading to deal closing or are about to enter the order-taking phase of your relationship. Be precise with your timing and remember, there is no limit to the

intensity of generosity a sentient client may experience, so don't hold back.

3. **Appearance.** Salespeople who converse in a calm but enthusiastic manner are most believed and respected. Do not be jittery or shift your eyes back-and-forth. A very slight pause before you respond to a question or conversation will reflect thoughtful attention. If a question is asked for which you do not know the answer, look the questioner in the eye and, in a (best as you can) truthful manner, explain that it is your (and our) sole intention to reduce the causes of suffering in his/her life, and regardless of what the correct answer might be, we are here to help achieve that objective. (And don't forget: the Buddha showed that a slight, beatific "power" smile goes a long way.)

There's more to come on this, for now let me be clear that we in the Executive Suite firmly believe that Lama Cheetem spoke for us all . . . there's much in the Buddhist teachings to lend prosperous direction and strength to our marketplace standing and success.

We are excited to introduce these ROI-rich, ground-breaking practices into our new-found (and deeply sincere) corporate consciousness.

• • •

One last thing. As has been the case since ancient days, those who are most committed to the Buddhist path awaken before sunrise and practice deep into the night.

Accordingly, we do believe that similar dedication on your part will lead to long-reaching success. So long-reaching that, upon death, those of you who are most diligent and committed to our corporate goals might find yourself propelled into the most precious of human rebirths ... destined to one day occupy your own office in our senior middle-management wing.

Remember, your clients are needy, and you are blessing them with access to our corporate bowl of perfect, wish-granting nectar. Use it in gobs to destroy any delays toward the realization of a revenue stream. Move them hard-and-fast to buy and you'll not only get their business, you'll have your company's deeply abiding love.

So, strive on with diligence. Remember, as Lama Cheetem said, "Mani brings money" so be sure to spread our special brand of enlightening bottom-line karma wherever you go.

Om Ah Ka-ching Hum!

Your tathagata, Chuck

-- Am stopping my finger now, thank you for reading. (2.20.13)

The UPS Sutra

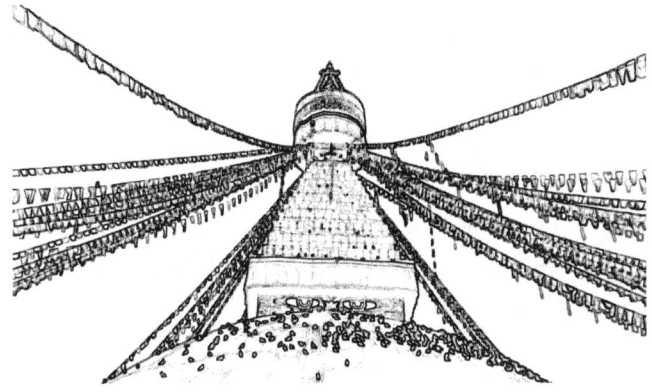

T hus I have heard.

The 21st Century Bodhisattva was sitting at home reading a collection of a friend's writings when she heard a knock at her door.

Looking through the window she saw the familiar brown truck parked outside; upon opening her door she was greeted by her local United Parcel Service delivery man. He gave her a small box, a book she had been expecting, and they exchanged pleasantries.

Concluding their conversation, she said as usual, "my gratitude to you and all the others who have made this possible."

Rather than turning and walking toward his truck, this time the man looked at her and asked, "You say that often. What do you mean when you say that . . . I've wondered . . . which others are you referring to?"

The Bodhisattva smiled, and as it was warm outside, invited the man in for some iced tea while she explained. After a brief hesitation, he accepted.

• • •

"Well," the Bodhisattva began, "I am appreciative to you for bringing this to my home, and also thankfully recognize all the others who played a role in the process."

"You mean our dispatchers and other drivers?"

"Well, yes, but there's many more . . . let's start at the beginning . . . hmm, well, actually, there is no beginning, as you'll soon see for yourself. As I've been anticipating reading the book you've just brought me, let's begin at its creation.

"I am most grateful to the book's author for writing it, and all those who made his life, experiences and writings possible . . . and then those who published it, making it available for distribution.

"Of course, its publication couldn't have occurred without the paper on which it is printed, so recognition and gratitude for all those who grew the trees, logged the lumber and made the paper is in order. And we mustn't forget those who built the machinery that enabled the paper to be made, and then those who got the paper to the printing plant, which was in turn created by many, many people. I acknowledge the role they all played, and thank them.

"Then there's the ink manufacturers, and those who made the crates for the ink and paper and books to be shipped in. We've already included many thousands of people, and we've only just produced the book . . . unmentioned are all the people, innumerable, who made it possible for those we've acknowledged to exist and to work. Each person, you know, had a vast web of support, both direct and indirect, that made their efforts possible.

"I recognize and thank them all.

"Since I ordered this book by computer from my local bookstore, there's all the people who made and make it possible for computers to exist, and for me to have one. Just think how many are responsible for getting electricity to our homes and places of business.

"And then there's the people at the bookstore, and those in the bank who created and operate the systems by which I could pay by using my account number . . . a remarkable amount of people.

"Each played a part in my having this book now . . . I recognize and thank them all."

. . .

Gesturing outside, the Bodhisattva continued, "Your truck . . .

all the materials and pieces that went into its construction, the designers and engineers and mechanics who put it together, and all those who discovered and drilled and refined the oil that became the gasoline that enabled you to get here today. I recognize and thank them.

"And there's you, not an independent entity but a product of infinite sources ... obviously there's your parents, made possible by their parents, and their parents ... and all the people who educated and nurtured you to the point of today being able to perform your work and knock on my door. Those who designed, harvested the materials and made the clothes you're wearing ... the food you've eaten, the bed you sleep in ... I recognize and thank them all.

"Do you realize how many people have played a role, through so many years and in so many places around the planet, leading to and culminating in this moment we are sharing here and now? And how if the contribution of just one of them didn't happen, or didn't occur in the way it did, how this moment could not have happened?

"Can you see the complete perfection of the vast and interdependent web in which we all live, in which we participate ... not just as a receiver but as a necessary contributor as well?

"This is what and whom I am acknowledging and offering gratitude for when I thank you and others ... and please understand that those "others" include all beings, not just those who are human."

The UPS man sat for a few moments in thought, and then

looked up. "Thank you. I always thought we were so singular, so alone . . . I never saw things in this way before . . . and it's all so . . . so unavoidably obvious.

"Thank you for showing me this, and for this refreshing drink, it was delicious." A small smile, "And thank you to all the beings who made this tea possible for me to enjoy. Thank you."

Then, remembering his work, he said, "I must be going now."

After saying goodbye, the man walked out toward his truck, his deepest perspectives expanding with each moment as he became increasingly aware of the timeless magnitude of the system in which he exists, in which all beings are included.

Deeply appreciative of his blossoming view, and thankful to the 21st Century Bodhisattva for sharing it with him, he climbed into his truck, started the engine and, smiling at the sheer vastness of it all, drove on to his next delivery.

-- Am stopping my finger now, thank you for reading.
(6.8.11)

Mind:
Past, Present and Future

The question was raised at a recent teaching; specifically what role does karma play in the determination of our rebirth or next life?

It came from a man who had been an Episcopal minister for 35 years, a thoughtful man who had, by virtue of how he posed his question, obviously put much thought into the various "what occurs after death?" scenarios.

We got around to answering the question, but were first led through the very interesting ground of ancestry. It was a discussion that can really test the limits of how much we as beginning Dharma students are really capable -- and willing -- to absorb.

Let's revisit . . .

. . .

These days many in our culture are spending significant time with ancestry, remembering and paying homage to predecessors: parents and grandparents, aunts and uncles, etc., getting a sense of who they really are in relation to the cultural family tree.

Ellis Island, just off the southern tip of Manhattan, is Ground Zero for a constant stream of visitors seeking to research their genealogy and learn more about their ancestral roots.

But Buddhism comes at who we are and from where we've come from a very different angle. Through the teachings on karma and rebirth, we see that physical ancestry plays a minimally direct role in terms of who and what I am today. Of much more significance are those unknown beings in which my mind was resident before taking rebirth in this incarnation.

Understand it this way: I am the karmic heir of the deeds of individuals who are long dead. The inclinations that propelled me into this wonderful life, to join with my parents and the conditions I was born into, were created by others . . . others for whom this mind, currently mine, was theirs.

Family history, etc? Yep, that's genetics, the DNA track, the material body and many of its "form" traits and conditions.

But the mind, infinite and formless, that through which every moment of consciousness is processed and experienced -- the essence of what I think is "me" -- was prepared and furnished to me through the efforts of those beings in whom it was previously resident.

It is they who earned this precious human life for whom I call me, it is they who paved the karmic path that I have undertaken to extend. It is they to whom I owe every bit of gratitude I can muster.

What a grand mystery! Who were these kind beings? Where and when did they live? How can I relate to them? Who was I before I was me? I have no direct experience of who or where these beings were . . . I know they were sentient, but other than that they remain completely unknown . . . but yet so connected.

There is no denying the precious gift of human rebirth and consciousness they have procured for this mind I now regard as mine.

So, with that said, are these untraceable "mind" ancestors more meaningful to me than my physical ancestors, including my parents?

That's hard to know; every mind needs a physical vehicle in which to function, and my material ancestors provided me with the composition of that. But as it is the mind through which I live, creating and experiencing absolutely everything via the aggregate of consciousness, the stage-setting contributions of my mind's previous 'owners' are certainly at least equally significant to those of my genetic ancestors.

Whoever and whatever they were.

• • •

Quiet down, sit for some moments, allowing the intense

"me-ness" to soften, and take a look at your life. Start at the beginning.

Let your imagination flow to consider how much of what you were born into and have continued to manifest is due to your mind's immediate predecessor and all of his or her forebearers. Trace the karmic chain, as you understand it, back to before your mind was yours.

Sit with this. And then, with awareness of the karma/rebirth workings in mind, bring it to the present day, and then stretch it out into the future . . . way past your present lifetime, your sense of "me".

Let your mind go beyond its borders, over the wall. Identify any sense of responsibility and magnanimity you might feel for the well-being of whoever your mind will next become.

Understand that as the process goes, one day someone else, some other being, will be the heir of your mind and its karma. The seeds of all your intentions, all your actions, the effects of absolutely everything you have done in this life in each and every moment will be born into someone else.

At the moment of your death, you will have spent a lifetime creating these karmic inclinations, and you're going to pass them onto someone else; a being who will then have what you've created, experience and revise it, and then pass that onto someone else upon their death.

This is the continuity of rebirth of which Buddhism informs us. Each moment of our life has a direct effect on the welfare of those with whom our mind will take residency after we are no longer able to physically support it . . . upon the death of our body.

It is all so very fantastic. Intentions extend reflections, so reflect. Appreciate your forebearers' incredibly precious mind-gift to you, and thank them by how and why you live each and every remaining moment of your life.

Do this for the benefit of those who will follow you.

Because they will.

-- Am stopping my finger now, thank you for reading. (7.16.12)

Emanations Everywhere

It was a small group to whom the 21st Century Bodhisattva spoke, her topic had been "The Mind." When she was done she asked if there were any questions.

A man named Chuck cleared his throat and asked, "Thank you so much for your talk, you've really captured my imagination, especially with your empowering way of describing how there are countless Buddhas throughout the universe continuously working for our benefit by emanating in every kind of way. I really love this idea, but am somewhat science-minded and don't think I've ever seen them, or have ever been aware of even one of them . . . can you talk some more of this?"

The Bodhisattva paused for a moment to collect her thoughts, smiled, and then began to speak.

• • •

"Well, the Buddhas don't always appear as Siddhartha did

in India 2,500 years ago. Upon achieving Buddhahood, i.e., uncovering the enlightenment at his mind's core, he became a wheel-turner, teaching the entire path of awakening to others. He needed to manifest as he did for best effectiveness, in order to "touch" as many people as he did. And so he took on the human persona of Siddhartha . . . the awakened one . . . the Buddha.

"So if you're looking for someone or something that looks like him, or resembles the Buddha you see represented in the various statues and graphics that seem to be everywhere these days, you're not likely to have much success.

"Usually, the Buddhas emanate in the most suitable ways to provide small indications of the path to individuals whose minds are receptive. They are in a sense experiential teaching moments, and they manifest in various manners, in any fashion actually . . . whatever is conducive to help bring about an instant of insight, realization or perhaps even awakening.

"These manifestations occur in an infinite variety of ways, often in physical form: as people or other beings, animate or inanimate objects. They could also be waves of sound, or certain aromas . . . beams of sunlight or beads of moisture. Anything that enters the mind's awareness through one of the sensory doors can be an emanation of the Buddhas . . . including thoughts and/or feelings.

"These Tathagata emanations are prodigious -- they're here, around at all times -- empowered by perfect wisdom and pure compassion, they are endless. The only thing that restricts them is our own narrow-mindedness, we are not always open to see or learn . . . and when our motivations are selfish their energy is obstructed.

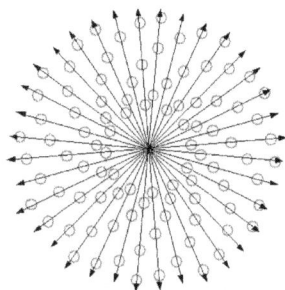

"To begin to see things in this way -- that anything and everything we encounter at each moment of consciousness is an enlightened emanation, what we refer to in Buddhism as a blessing, there for us to benefit from if we just recognize it to be so -- is perhaps one of the most profound insights one experiences on the spiritual path.

• • •

"Let me recount a story. The great scholar and meditator Asanga lived and practiced in a cave for twelve years, trying to see Maitreya, the future Buddha. He had no success, and on several occasions he almost gave up. Finally, after 12 years he was done trying.

"While walking along the road back to his village, he came across a brown dog with a rapidly fouling wound full of maggots on its back. Feeling unbearable compassion for this suffering dog, he decided to clean the wound but realized that if he used a stick it would not only hurt the maggots but they would no longer have anything to eat.

"Selflessly, he cut off a piece of his own flesh and then tried to move the maggots from the dog to the piece of flesh. So as not to hurt them, he opted to use his moist, soft tongue to transport them.

"As the sight and smell of the wound were terribly repulsive, he closed his eyes and held his breath as he stuck his tongue out and leaned towards the dog's wound . . . but strangely, as he kept leaning forward there was nothing there.

"Confused, he opened his eyes to see the dog had become Maitreya Buddha.

"'Where have you been?' asked a confused Asanga. 'For twelve years I have been trying to see you, and now you are here.'

"Maitreya replied, 'I was in your cave all the time, in the corner where you spat after clearing your throat.' He showed Asanga his cloak which was covered in dry spittle. 'But after so long, this is a new day. It is the great compassion you have just manifested that has enabled you to see me.'

"Asanga was so happy that he ran toward and through the village carrying Maitreya on his shoulders, shouting, 'Look, look! Everyone come out, come out! Maitreya Buddha is here!'

"The people came out of their homes but could not see Maitreya. In fact, all they saw was a crazy man running down the street. One old lady who used to recite the mantra Om Mani Padme Hum with faith but no understanding saw a man carrying a brown dog on his back."

. . .

Moments of silence as the 21st Century Bodhisattva looked into the eyes of those gathered around her. "You see, from our side, the mind must be open and able to see the Buddhas who are there all the time even though we do not yet have the merit to see them. This is why we study and contemplate the pith instructions of our lineage teachers, work to identify and clarify the "natural state" of mind in our meditation practices, and cultivate renunciation of the causes of dukkha."

As understanding dawned on the faces of her listeners, she concluded, "It is excellent preliminary mind training to always be aware the Buddhas are nearby. It will help make us mindful and careful in our actions. This is not fantasy . . . the minds of the Buddhas are omniscient, they see everything and are always present, inside and out."

In a soft voice Chuck added, "Yes, and we'd better be careful where we spit."

Nods and smiles . . . a significant Dharma instruction had been shared, it was now to be contemplated and understood as the capacity of each of the participants allows.

The group draws in closer as another question is asked . . .

-- Am stopping my finger now, thank you for reading. (9.2.2015)

Note: The story of Asanga comes from Thubten Gyatso (Dr. Adrian Feldman); shared here with gratitude and wishes for benefit for all.

"I Want to Learn How to Meditate"

I was at my desk when my mobile phone "binged" announcing a new text message. It was from my daughter Claire, a senior in high school, and her message was straight-forward. "I want to learn how to meditate," it said.

I texted back "why" and she said she just had "a couple of very interesting and profound conversations with some friends."

I asked her to call me, she responded she would after eating lunch.

Claire, along with my other children, doesn't live with me, but she has spent much time at my home. Over the years she's become quite familiar with Tibetan Buddhist images and icons ... she understands and enjoys the thangkas and prayer flags and malas and incense, my stories of India and a variety of other associated things. And while numerous seeds have naturally planted, I've not manipulated or pressured her (or them) in any way to pursue Dharma.

As I waited for her call, I gathered some thoughts and ideas. I'll probably not share these with Claire so soon, but will be mindful of them while we speak. Here are some . . .

· · ·

Meditation is, among many other things, a wonderful way of learning how our mind works, and in terms of living with clarity and well-being, it is one of the very best things we can do.

Gom, the Tibetan word that means meditation, translates more accurately to "familiarize." Additionally, the Tibetan word for "Buddhist" is *nangpa*, which means "insider" -- someone who seeks the truth not outside but within the nature of his or her mind.

Most Westerners equate mind with thinking, but in Buddhism it is acknowledged to be much more . . . mind is the entire spectrum of our inner experiences: thoughts, feelings, perceptions, consciousness, subconsciousness, unconsciousness . . . much more than just our thoughts. Mind is the basis of our entire experience . . . our perceiver, translator, reflector and mirror. Without it there is nothing. Every moment of which we are aware, every concept we have, every aspect of our sense of self, anything and everything that "is" comes to us through the (at its core) clear, brilliant, multi-faceted jewel that is our mind.

To begin a meditation practice is to learn how to observe the mind, and at some point a small-at-first awakening occurs . . . an awakening to a profound understanding.

Referred to by some as an "aha" moment, it's as if we've

been living in a small, windowless room for our entire life, comfortable and fairly satisfied with what the room contains.

Then one day a window appears and opens. Gazing out for the first time, there's so much to see, so much there . . . vastly more than what we've been told and led to believe there is, or could be.

At that moment, our little room, which encompassed everything of which we were ever aware, becomes just a little room, and our relationship to everything inside (and now outside as well) changes . . . including, most significantly, the relationship we have with ourself.

Once we have this view, we're never the same again. (Nor would most want to be.)

This awakening is a result of meditation.

• • •

The philosopher George Gurdjieff wrote that in order to become free, one must first understand that he or she is in prison. So it is with our minds as well.

We may think and believe we are free because we can do so many different things: many of us can have nearly anything we want, can go where we'd like, can read and write and eat when we want, can speak freely.

We might like to think we're free, it's a nice thought . . . but this freedom is confined within narrow self-made parameters. And once we begin to sit, breathe and look inside, this all becomes very clear.

Our mind churns anger and attachment and aversion . . . fear, doubt, worries and arrogance . . . jealousies and self-centeredness . . . all swirling about, in and out of our thoughts, intentions and actions. To see and understand this is to realize that as long as our mind is clouded by the ignorance that allows these states of mind to arise, yanking us back and forth, we are not really free . . . could never be free.

We are living our life under the control of confusing misunderstandings and delusions in partnership with the unending parade of our afflictive emotions, and there is no freedom there.

"Ah, the human condition!" you might say.

Perhaps, but not necessarily so. Because sometimes a path of self-discovery appears, inviting us to sit and watch and listen and learn and understand. Emerging from long-held misunderstandings and confusion, in clarity we find true freedom.

. . .

A meditation practice fosters a healthy curiosity which often leads to the Dharma, and then the path truly unfolds. It can be a gnarly path, challenging at times, demanding honesty and hard work . . . but it leads to wonderful rewards.

Our mind is the ongoing stream basis of who and what we are.

With meditation it becomes infused with unbinding insights bringing about generosity, patience, confidence and joy. All of which leads to increasingly potent purpose and strength.

These mind states then enrich virtue and well-being and the blossoming of wisdom, the fountainhead of compassionate intentions and actions that become the causes of true happiness.

Meditation is a key component in this process, which brings about the highest and most effective remedy to our delusions, the purest state of mind: bodhichitta.

This is our most profound, clearest, most brilliant nature, beyond which there is no greater virtue . . . bodhichitta, simplicity within exquisite beauty: the mind that intuitively and skillfully takes others in care more than oneself.

. . .

Those on the Mahayana path have come to experience bodhichitta's awakening in many different ways, at different times, in different places.

Perhaps even starting with a text message from a daughter to her dad that says "I want to learn how to meditate."

-- Am stopping my finger now, thank you for reading.
(1.12.11)

The Future of
American Enlightenment

Being a news-aware resident of Washington State, it is hard to escape the intensifying buzz of medical and recreational cannabis.

Hemp festivals abound, featuring vendors of just about every green device or seed in existence, all exploring business-to-business networking opportunities and offering information to those looking to merge marijuana consumption (technically THC with all the derivative oils and waxes and edibles now), with yoga, vegan eating, topical ointments, sex lubricants and grass-roots political activism.

Kathy and I recently attended Seattle's Hemp Cup, an event sponsored by a national magazine and held at a large arena on the outskirts of the city. It was a circus-like atmosphere featuring live music, parties, cannabis taste/potency competitions, seminars, a vendor expo and lots of people -- predominantly youthful -- most being imbibers with others (like us) passing through more out of curiosity.

While there was much to see, what captured my keen attention was a booth near the rear of the exhibit hall with a large Buddha statue on the table and posters announcing the "Bodhi-Patch ... for Instant Enlightenment -- Anytime, Anywhere, Anyone."

I had to investigate.

. . .

The booth was peopled by a young couple in tie-dyed OM t-shirts and baseball caps, pulsating mandalas on their laptop screens and beatific smiles on their faces.

"Hi," I said. "I'm interested in what you've got here."

"Well, I'm glad you stopped by," the man jumped up and we shook hands. "My name is Samadhi, and this is my lady Divine."

Divine smiled and flashed a peace sign.

"What we've got is a perfect blend of easy-to-achieve spiritualism and THC buzz-feed ... the Bodhi-Patch, the easy means to instant bud-blast-off enlightenment."

"Yeah, and not just enlightenment, but wisdom, bliss, compassion and even some know-it-all omniscience -- you know, all that Buddhist stuff that's getting so popular these days," Divine added, pointing toward an old photo of the Dalai Lama hanging crookedly on their booth's back curtain.

"Wow, that's fantastic," I said, incredulous I was hearing and seeing this. "So, how does it work?"

"Well, it's simple," Samadhi said, reaching below the table and producing a small plastic bag containing what looked like a thick, circular pad about two inches in diameter, saffron in color with a black Buddha outline sitting on a bright green marijuana leaf at its center.

"Here it is, one of the last I have left. They've been flying out of here. Pure solvent-based extracts, a minimum of 55 percent THC for the head -- er, I mean mind, and 14 percent Cannabidiol for body relaxation. Both soaked into a transdermal self-stick patch and absorbed through your skin like water into a sponge.

"The result: mind and body in perfect harmony, yin and yang entwined, floating gently on the stream of your awakened consciousness. Simply peel off the back and stick the patch firmly on your skin. Some people like to place it on a chakra point, others prefer the soft spot just behind the ear -- but anywhere will do. Once it's in place, you just relax and let it do its thing."

"And what exactly is 'its thing'?" I asked.

"Ahhh, its thing is simply the greatest spiritual reality to ever hit the market, the perfect merging of the high and the deep. It provides all the beauty of awakened higher mind states without the time-consuming process of learning how to cultivate them.

"It's a simple and easy bypass to the long process of spiritual study and meditation, which so many of us just can't stick with. You know, we Americans don't do so well with baby steps, we're just not wired with patience for that ancient, long-range stuff. We like our short-cuts."

Samadhi smiled, "I noticed you're walking with a light limp. For people whose knees have become tender and painful from too much meditation sitting, I tell them to put a patch on each knee -- bingo, it really makes the point!"

Divine nodded in agreement, "Yeah, meditators and all those people getting involved in Buddhism work so hard to experience enlightenment, but even if they can feel some it's so limited -- whatever they get is only in their mind. With our patches, once the mojo is absorbed, enlightenment flows through every nook and cranny of the body -- it's part of your blood, it's you!"

Samadhi chimed in, "You know, our Bodhi-Patches are truly revolutionary, a modern-day miracle. They're perfect for our busy lives -- just stick one on and in a few moments you're there: the bliss-place, the exquisite one-ness spiritual seekers, meditators and yes, drug users have been trying to get to for thousands of years . . . perfect non-duality, liberation from the hum-drum, unbounded freedom, love for everyone.

"It's absolutely perfect enlightenment. It's explosive . . . a buzz that blows the head open!"

Back to Divine. "Yes, and to heighten the pleasure, based on our dedication to providing the ultimate customer experience, our patches come in wonderful time-release aromas. We call them our 'Shangri-La Scents'... we've got Tibetan Butter Tea, Ganges Ganja, Paramita Poppy and, for animal lovers, or those who just want to mix a little wildlife into their high-altitude awakening, we're about to release our next scent, Chomolungma Yak."

"And of course, all our scents are made of mostly organic ingredients," Samadhi proudly added.

• • •

At first I thought this booth, the whole idea, the whole thing, was a creative part of Hemp Cup entertainment, that Samadhi and Divine were a couple of actors in vendor drag. Then I had the notion I was part of some hidden camera routine, which would be revealed at any moment.

But before long I got it: this product and these people were for real. And I confess that I wanted to play along for just a bit longer.

Looking from one to the other, "Wow. You two have thought of everything. How long do your patches last for, what's the duration of their effect?"

Divine responded, "We use only the highest concentrations of THC, so your high, er, uh, enlightenment will last for about three hours."

"Ok, that sounds good. How much does a patch cost?"

Samadhi answered, "Well, we have a starter kit that costs $89.99. It includes three patches, your choice of scents and a one-month subscription to our proprietary website -- BodhiPatch.com -- where we stream music and videos especially attuned to produce realizations designed to work with and enhance your enlightenment experience."

Divine bubbled, "We've got a mobile app version of the website coming out next week. Buy now, and, as a Hemp Cup show attendee," she winked, "unlimited VIP access is included in your package price."

Okay, I had had enough. "Well," I said, "thank you both for the explanation. A pot-induced enlightenment in a skin patch sounds amazing. I just don't think I'm ready for something like this yet. I don't ... "

Samadhi leaned forward and cut me off. "Whoa! Listen man, turn around and look at all these people, have some clear vision. It's a beautiful Saturday afternoon and they're jammed inside here. It's all about cannabis ... see it straight-out ... you're looking at the beginnings of the most profound development in American consciousness history."

Excitement in his voice. "In the days ahead weed and its derivatives are going to be legal everywhere, and we've got the spiritual angle all figured out. Getting high, getting enlightened ... the two together are naturals, like cream cheese and jelly, day and night, yin and yang. This is huge!

"And by bringing this technology to the masses, I am the future. Bodhi Patches will be worn by people in their living rooms and bedrooms, their workplaces, hospitals, places of worship -- everywhere. Our marketplace ranges from the most serious of spiritual seekers all the way to those simply looking for an occasional, easy, feel-good technique. They'll be used during childbirth, kids will be raised with them, the dying will die with them. Really, there's no end to it, or the money we'll make!"

Samadhi removed his cap for a moment and ran his fingers through his hair as if cultivating a brainstorm. After a few moments back went the cap, followed by a subtle nod, signaling he had come to an important decision.

"I'll tell you what: buy a couple of starter kits now, see how you like being enlightened, and when it works for you get back to me. Maybe you can become one of my regional distributors! I'm going to make tons of money in this industry for a lot of years to come . . . Bodhi Patches are coming strong, and I AM Bodhi Patches. Like I said before, I am the future. You can be a small part of it . . . how many starter kits do you want?"

"How old are you?" I was curious.

"Nearly twenty-two," grinned the future of American enlightenment.

-- Am stopping my finger now, thank you for reading. (10.20.14)

Garden of Mind

"Whatever kind of seed is sown in a field, prepared in due season, a plant of that same kind, marked with the peculiar qualities of the seed, springs up from it."
  -- Guru Nanak
     (founder of Sikhism and the first of the Sikh Gurus)

This week, after almost two years of weekly Lam-rim Chen-mo study, we at Chenrezig Project formally entered Je Tsongkhapa's Great Scope teachings. Following a discussion of the conditions, causes and strengths of the mind in which bodhicitta arises, we shared in a short Tonglen meditation.

As many know, Tonglen is the Mahayana compassion practice of "taking and giving" -- i.e., meditatively taking on the suffering of others, by which we diminish and shatter our sense of self-cherishing, and then visualizing selflessly giving to those others all the ingredients necessary to relieve the suffering we've taken on.

For some in attendance, this was a first Tonglen meditation, others were quite experienced. At its conclusion we briefly discussed what just occurred in the practice, coming to an understanding that, even if there was just a fleeting moment of the realization of courageously kind "taking and giving" – for example, taking on others' hunger and thirst and giving back nourishment -- that a very precious seed planted in each of our mind-streams. And, as Guru Nanak states in the quote above, that seed will blossom with its content being of the "same nature" of mind when the conditions are right for it do so.

So, yes, an inclination or seed of selflessness and (resulting) compassion is planted in the mind, and within that seed is the potential for many moments of selflessness, wise compassion, inexhaustible loving kindness.

It is in this way that we are, at all times, architecting the experiences of our future moments.

As one orange seed yields a tree of oranges, with each crop then yielding countless seeds, virtuous inclinations planted in the mind during a transformative meditative practice such as Tonglen ultimately blossom into mind moments of profound benefit. Such is the nature of seeds, in which is already present the qualities resident within the ripened fruit to be.

Do the work. Study, ponder, meditate. Set intentions and then skillfully act to bring them to life. Plant virtuous, wide-reaching inclinations in your mind-stream ... from which, regardless in your current situation, will blossom understandings and realizations leading to well-being born of wisdom and compassion.

So beneficial. So precious.

-- Am stopping my finger now, thank you for reading.
(4.28.10)

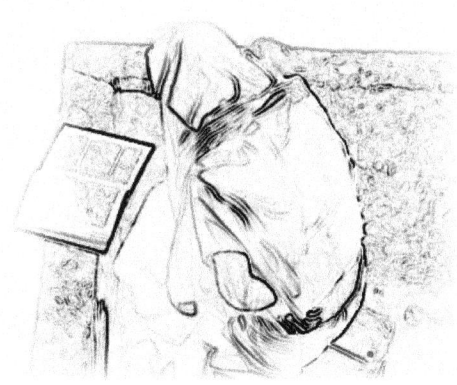

The Abbot of Ghoom

"Please tell us a little of your teachers."

The request was made at the conclusion of the 21st Century Bodhisattva's teaching on "Karma and Lineage" and came from a young man seated in the front row.

It was a request that took her by surprise. Once heard, pure beauty exploded in her mind, so rich have the experiences of her teachers been . . . and continue to be.

She thanked the man for his request, referencing the preciousness she had been asked to share. Then, in a soft voice she began.

"Well, we've all had many significant teachers; quite often they appear in our lives not with a formal title or bearing the obvious signs of a teacher. In fact, sometimes we initially perceive them as not so beneficial, initially regarding them as troublesome, presenting unnecessary challenges or difficulties.

"But, afterwards, with reflection, we often see that the insights and understandings they've guided us toward are favorably relevant and meaningful . . . wholesome learning experiences . . . often just what we needed at the time.

"Of the many, for me the one who jumps to mind most clearly is the first person I encountered as a direct, personal teacher of the Dharma: a wonderful lama known as Dhardo Rinpoche. He was the abbot of Ghoom Monastery, set off from the tea estates on the outskirts of the West Bengali (India) mountain town of Darjeeling.

"I was in the Himalayas as a tourist, and had gone to visit the monastery with the hopes of taking some photos of authentic Buddhist monks . . . little did I know what I was walking into."

"I was invited to sit and watch an afternoon practice that was taking place in the old monastery's gompa, or prayer hall. It was exotic and mysterious. I remember the gompa as being the first place in which I ever saw a large statue of the Buddha . . . it was so beautiful. There was lots of chanting and energetic noise-making, all done with a clear sense of joy.

The practice ended after about two hours, and as I was leaving an English-speaking monk approached and told me that Rinpoche welcomes me to return as I may.

"I did not know who Rinpoche was, but I soon found out.

• • •

"My visits to the monastery became regular, and in time I began to feel comfortable there, no longer a tourist but a familiar guest. Amid all the beauty of the surroundings and the prayers and chants of the monks, and in spite of the difficult taste of yak-butter tea [laughing], I began to be fascinated by -- and drawn to -- Dhardo Rinpoche.

"His allure was so beautiful, so strong. It wasn't any one thing he did, just simply all he was.

"Rinpoche had such a wise and gentle manner about him, and even though he spoke only Tibetan, the things I learned by just being around and watching him were empowering . . . so simply, beautifully, humanly empowering.

"For example, the way he was with the people who came to him -- not only his monks, for whom he served as teacher, spiritual mentor and oftentimes father -- but also the people of the community. Every day there would be visitors seeking his guidance, and even in his elderly years he never appeared too tired or busy to welcome and serve them joyously.

"The way he would look upon people . . . strength and softness shining from his eyes . . . and the nurturing kindness in his expressions ... how he would gently lean forward to cup their faces, and hold them close to his heart.

"Sometimes his embrace would last for minutes, with each of them softly crying ... and then often giggling together.

"He was so open, so sensitive to others. But make no mistake, there was nothing malleable or mushy about Rinpoche. In everything he did, and whoever he was with, there was a natural dignity and inspiring sense of no-nonsense about him.

"I watched him closely and while I couldn't understand his words, his mannerisms were unmistakable -- I never saw him flatter anyone, heap praise on them, or criticize or chastise ... and with his own disciples he seemed particularly uncompromising in ensuring they never tended toward lazy behavior, words or thoughts.

"Rinpoche's ability to guide others by sharing himself was an unsurpassable blessing for all ... I believe he was acutely aware of this, as he was of the profound beauty of his work.

• • •

"What occurred in that monastery, Rinpoche's monastery, was completely new to me. I had never been in a place like that, nor had I ever seen anyone be that way with others, I hadn't known it was possible. To say that it changed my perspectives on who and what a human being is capable of is ... well, let's just say that's an understatement.

"I remember how, day after day, I wanted nothing more than

simply to remain in his presence, watching him, learning from him … perhaps one day even beginning to be like him.

"He was my first teacher of the Buddhist ways, He opened my mind and touched my heart … he was for me, at that time and in that place, perfect."

"As I sit here today, miles and years removed from those days in Ghoom, there are many precious Dhardo Rinpoche "mind morsels" that, apparently deeply planted, continue to sprout and blossom wherever I am."

With folded hands brought to her chest in gratitude, "Perhaps you can sense the joyful energy this provides.

"Such is the nature of the Buddhist teachings and the authentic teachers who share them; rarely are their words facts or absolute statements. Rather they are powerful seeds that embed in the mind, arising as guiding insights and realizations in the most opportune moments for them to do so.

"Hence, the incalculable benefits of paying attention to our teachers at all times with a focused, open and penetrable mind."

· · ·

The Bodhisattva took a sip of her tea, glanced at her questioner and continued.

"Once again, thank you for your question. Perhaps in days to come I'll relate specific tales of Rinpoche to further illustrate the topics we're discussing. It will be a joy to do so, there are so many instances, I will try my best to pass along essence examples of his wisdom, grace and beauty.

"But now, in conclusion, I'd like to leave you with one of the simplest yet most treasured perspectives of the enlightened view I've encountered through the years. Presented by different teachers in many diverse circumstances . . . each time clear and pointed . . . and deeply freeing . . .

"Our lives are not, as we often think of them, too-brief flashes of independent self-first "being" on this living planet.

"Rather, every one of us -- all beings -- are interdependently connected by an elaborate network of infinite causes and conditions . . . all of which were occurring well before our existence and will continue long after our current lives are over. We are here by the ongoing grace of those conditions, and everything we do manifests as a categorical result of them.

"With each instant of our lives we and all other beings are actively contributing to this perpetual tapestry, blueprinting future repercussions upon which each of us, along with absolutely everything else, has an impact.

"Ponder this. Snuggle up to it. Be honest and fearless in your considerations, and pay attention to where it leads you . . . likely to humility born of a "seeing" of vast inter-connectedness and, yes, empowering responsibility to everyone and everything around you.

"This is where the curriculum of Mahayana teachings, from all teachers, leads . . . awakened beings having turned away from the narrow, self-based urgings of their own egocentric ideas and inclinations . . . re-seeing, rethinking and readjusting their own existence within the larger context of a timeless, interdependent community."

. . .

The 21st Century Bodhisattva paused for a few moments, allowing the vision to penetrate.

"Consider this viewpoint. Sit quietly with it. Be patient, allow your mind to open. Explore its vastness as best you can . . . then allow your discoveries to lead you to do and be what you will.

"That's right . . . let me say it again . . . quiet down, open, explore, discover . . . and then do and be what you will.

"In essence, this was the root of all the teaching and activities of Dhardo Rinpoche, the abbot of a hallowed Buddhist monastery in India's Himalaya . . . a man whose greatness was completely in accord with the teachings he offered.

"He of simple and beautiful ways, who taught by splendid example . . . a precious teacher.

"It has been my pleasure to introduce him to you."

-- Am stopping my finger now, thank you for reading.
(10.14.15)

The Journey Is the Prize

A recent Chenrezig Project gathering became a Dharma potpourri ... as soft mountain rain fell outside, we ventured from meditation to a discussion on impermanence and then to the two accumulations of the Buddhist path (merit and wisdom).

Our discussion on wisdom seemed particularly full-toned, I'd like to share some of our notions herein ...

Tibetan Buddhism leads us to see and understand that, in each moment, all things (including each of us) are:
1. completely dependent on their parts (which are completely dependent on their parts, etc.);
2. interrelated, not isolated and;
3. moment-by-moment combinations of causes and conditions; merely labelled by mind.

Through Buddhism we're also guided to deter and ultimately correct habitual misunderstanding(s), turning away from the extreme beliefs that:

1. any or all things are permanent (i.e., unchanging), existing or occurring independent of their parts (and of our labeling), and that;

2. the perspective of "ultimate reality" confirms that things do not really exist at all (i.e., the mistaken nihilistic view, a common initial misconception in the "emptiness" teachings).

At the outset, most of us see the Buddhist curriculum's "wisdom" ideas in a purely conceptual manner, but in time they reveal undeniable logic and practicality. Study and honest engagement then serve to deepen our understandings, bringing to the forefront encouraging ways in which we perceive the world and our infinite relationships with it.

As we distill and integrate these understandings into our real-time perspectives and viewpoints, a progressive series of profound and empowering -- and yes, practical -- wisdom-instilled "action-oriented insights" comes to life. Intuitive within our mind's operating system, they abide in our mental here-and-now and influence everything we do and experience.

• • •

Here are some of the ways these wisdom insights relate to whatever it is we call "I" and "me" and "mine"...

I understand that:

- I am never isolated from my surroundings and other living beings, but am (at all times) a participating aspect of a vast and perfect web of interconnections and interdependence.

- I "create" and experience every characteristic of the world through my own concepts and ideas.

- At all times, everything within and outside of me is changing ... causes combine and create effects which then become causes combining into new effects, whether I am aware of this ongoing process or not. With this, my mind, including whatever it is processing, adapts in concert.

- My identity, my personality, my essence, my soul ... the preciousness of me, myself and I ... my "is-ness" ... is a persistent exercise in illusion. How I experience and relate to the world is occurring through a self-distorted set of personal beliefs and perspectives about fundamental aspects of reality that ground and influence all my perceiving, thinking and knowing. In other words, my views and experiences of reality -- the essence of my consciousness -- depends on my own ideas/projections .. incorrectly fueled and complicated by identification with my ego.

- Accordingly, this world and every moment in it is "my" film, "my" projection ... and because I produce, direct and star in my show, and the cameras are always running, I alone have the ability and responsibility to create my experience(s) of the world ... but for true accuracy and beauty, the lens of my camera must be clear and it's inner workings (i.e., my mind) must be free of impediments and misapprehensions.

- My mind is mutable ... "I" is only a label, a concept ... impermanent and dependent on an ongoing stream of causes and conditions, just like all phenomena.

Readied with the vigor of these understandings and the confidence they cultivate, we study, contemplate and meditate. Then, affirming the empowering new perspectives that emerge, we engage in the challenges and opportunities our lives present.

This is the path of accumulated wisdom, the path of Buddhist practice ... the path leading away from ignorant self-centeredness and toward true virtue and happiness. It is a path of honesty -- beautiful, challenging, scary at times, and always beneficial. Traveling it requires effort and the courage to leave behind once-comfortable but now increasingly obsolete habits and routines.

...

This world is a wondrous place, keenly fruitful beyond ordinary perceptions. Allow your imagination to see it as it appears to the purely healthy and clear mind ... a place where flowers blossom with the sights and scents of compassion ... where teachings of selflessness emerge from the singing wings of cicadas ... where from the nighttime crickets come rhythmic songs of companionship and amity.

It's a world where tiny, melodious bells hang from gently swaying trees, filling the air with the sweet, tinging sounds of Dharma.

Here rain drops fall from pastel skies, carrying legions of tiny

Buddhas ... cascading on sentient beings and their habitats, each drop exploding into beneficial emanations; soaking, being absorbed ... harmonious Buddha whispers in every language known to beings, songs of impermanence ... loving-kindness ... generosity ... patience ... virtue ... enthusiasm ... joy.

An environment where absolutely everything in and about it -- whether seen, smelled, heard, felt, tasted or thought -- is a teaching of liberation, freedom and enlightenment, intuitively understood and motivational to all.

. . .

Yes, I am aware this may sound like a stretch, some type of fantasy or daydream, or perhaps just some eager metaphor for wishfully conjuring an over-the-top viewpoint of a fantastic paradise ... itself illusory; an unreal place, an impossible state of mind. But if you're reading this, perhaps there's an inkling, a sense there's more here than just some whimsical ramblings.

And, seeking to learn more, your studies begin.

The word used to describe this is wisdom. It points to much, including the awakened understanding of how you and everything around you occurs, and always has ... in ways brilliant, uncontaminated, free of confusion, unmistakably clear.

This is where the remarkable path of Buddhist sensibilities, practices and activities leads ... to an awakened presence revealed by replacing long-standing misunderstandings with accumulated insight ... to riches of mind not acquired or created but rather uncovered from within.

It is a reality so intuitively correct and freeing that, upon encountering it, your only remaining element of disbelief will be wonder at how you could have been ignorant of its presence for so long.

. . .

The perfectly flawless, infinitely-faceted diamond mind is resident deeply within all sentient beings. Many are aware of its presence, perhaps you are one of them.

It is there waiting to blossom, as it has been for countless lifetimes. We simply embark on the Dharma path, trek, awaken and transform.

The journey toward it is the prize . . . along the way, everything changes in the very best of ways.

-- Am stopping my finger now, thank you for reading. (11.11.15)

"There's Nothing Magical About This..."

It was a larger than usual crowd for the teaching, and as it ended a young man who had been coming to gatherings for a few weeks came toward the 21st Century Bodhisattva.

Awkward as he approached, there was an underlying directness to him of which she took note. After exchanging pleasantries, he shared his concerns.

"I've been attending your teachings for a while now, and have to say most of what I hear resonates with me and is useful in some of the things in my life right now... but something is missing.

"There's this nagging question, 'What do I want?... What do I truly want'? that I struggle with. The truth is, it's slippery.

"There are things, and even some people I have in my life now don't satisfy me anymore, in fact they often annoy and seem to confine me.

"And even when I think about changing them, there's nothing I can visualize pursuing that wouldn't be more trouble or effort than it could be worth.

"I find this is true with my work, my relationships, my entertainments and just about everything else . . . things that used to seem so easy . . . it has all become so challenging.

"I listened carefully to your teaching on Impermanence and Emptiness last week, and thought for a while that a grasp of that might be helpful in finding an answer, but I couldn't get past how anything that's empty could be satisfying?

"Not only can't I get my arms around this, more and more there's a desperate sense I really need to figure it out in order to pull myself together.

"How can I know what I truly want when everything is changing at each moment, including my flip-flopping mind . . . the basis of my entire experience?"

He looked at the Bodhisattva with a wry smile, "Do you have any advice for me?"

After a few moments she began to speak.

• • •

"You bring to mind the 5th Century monk Bodhidharma, who when asked the question 'Who are you?'-- which I believe is akin to 'What do I want?' -- answered 'I don't know' . . . this was his answer to that question, repeatedly, wherever he went.

"It's interesting, because when you truly -- and I say 'truly' meaning only after honest investigation -- don't know who you are, or as you say, 'know what you want', you can experience a wonderful, disentangling state of desirelessness . . . a state of being so freeing that many people actually become uncomfortable -- even frightened -- about approaching it.

"You see, many of us feel very secure within our fetters."

The man frowned, questioning, as the Bodhisattva continued.

• • •

"There are some progressive steps in the process which I believe get us closer to a clear understanding of what we really want, which for most of us is simply to be happy . . . to experience the mind that arises through increasingly consistent well-being.

"At first, we don't know what we truly want because we haven't really thought about it very much. Many people find themselves in this stage, carelessly reacting to what is occurring around them, bouncing back and forth with very little guiding awareness or mindfulness of direction or path.

"Then, as we do begin to think about it, our thoughts emerge outward from a seeking-to-be-satisfied sense of self, with our habitual thinking filled with 'I want this' or 'I want that' or 'I want the other one' etc.

"Desires erupt, an unending array, really. What we want and perceive we need, always swirling. And then there's what we don't want, version is also a desire.

"But some eventually get beyond that; as they really think about their intentions from a vaster perspective, they come to the understanding that, 'well, no, I don't really want this or that ... I might be satisfied with it for awhile, and I wouldn't turn my nose up at it, but I don't think it's really what I want, nor is it anything I need.'

"And why is this? Two reasons.

"First, we may find that in some ways we already have access to the same essence we perceive our 'wants' would bring, in other words, it's been there -- we've had it all along.

"Second, we've begun to doubt the "for me" benefits of what we want because we're no longer sure of what or who we are. And many of us, most of us in fact, never take the time to truly learn what we need to learn in order to know ourselves."

She looked toward the man and spoke softly.

"A knife can't cut itself, fire doesn't burn itself and light can't illuminate itself. Without making the effort to peer behind our own curtain into the backstage of our mind, we can only be a mystery to ourselves."

. . .

A few moments as this resonated, and then the man asked, "This aspect of my mind that is mystery, how do I get to know it . . .?"

"Careful investigation, honest introspection and meditation lead us there. And not rejecting but embracing this 'I don't know' -- when felt from the depths, whispered deeply in the mind, is the same thing as 'I love, I don't try to force or control'. It brings a spacious -- and increasingly fearless -- humility.

"You see, the Buddha taught that when we cease grasping for control we're able to emerge from the confusion of insecurity that causes that clinging. And when we cease to cling, we break through to a tremendous source of clear strength and energy . . . that which arises from our own mind.

"It's the nectar of awakening, now flowing through all we are . . . we've been habitually blocking it, wasting energy in our many forms of continuous self-defense. The moment we stop doing that it's all there for us . . . brilliant and empowering.

"And who we've thought we are and what we've thought we want becomes completely meaningless, nothing more than tired labels and concepts of control, the fodder of long-held, stubborn limitations.

"This is what's meant by the Dharma slogan, 'The more we surrender, the more we have.'"

• • •

Feeling stirrings of understanding, the man looked down at the Bodhisattva's folded hands, hesitated for a moment and said, "I believe I hear what you're saying and it sounds wonderful, but . . . but I don't think I have the courage to give my desire for control away."

The Bodhisattva smiled, "Of course you don't, not yet. From

our ordinary vantage point very few do. But please consider that need for control to be nothing more than a blockage to the richness of your mind . . . a dead-end. Grow tired and bored of it . . . allow it to cease.

"The Buddha's great teachings on impermanence speak to this. Everything, including each of us, is merely occurring, a transitory 'happening'.

In the nature of occurrence it and we are all moving moment-by-moment through the unstoppable process of aging, maturing, decaying and ultimately falling apart.

"This perspective into the workings of compositional arisings -- of which everything is an aspect -- is foundational in Buddhist thought and practice. I believe your spending some time with it will be of assistance to you."

The man leaned in closer.

"The fact that everything is in flux; always changing, coming together and falling apart . . . this is your helper . . . it reveals that you don't have to try to let go, because there's really nothing so enduring that it can be held on to.

"This is the natural process, see it. You don't have to become anyone new, do anything dramatically different or go to a foreign country or culture to see it. It is in play everywhere you are, the dance of the forces of dependent origination and impermanence . . . it is the ongoing reality in which you, nature and everything else are interdependently encompassed.

"You merely have to know it.

"When you attain this view from the inside -- not as a spectator but as a participant -- everything changes. You suddenly find you have strength ... an enormous torrent of energy, astoundingly deep and powerful.

"It is an energy of love and kindness, compassion and equanimity, great patience, generosity and moral certitude. It's not one day found and hooked into but was always there, resident in your mind, just waiting to be uncovered and experienced.

"It blossoms along with a deep sense of confidence and understanding, you'll intuitively trust it, and it will always be there for you. There's nothing magical about this ... it will not immediately remove all your conflicts by erasing troublesome situations, but will motivate and empower you to resolve them in the most virtuous and healthy of ways.

"As is the case with all significant transformation, there may initially be some doubt or uncertainty, but it will vanish as morning dew disappears in the sun's warmth. You'll no longer question or wonder about yourself, you'll know ... this is who you truly are.

"Trust that it is there, dwelling, native to your mind, ready to arise ... this was Siddhartha's great discovery on the evening of his enlightenment."

Enough had been said. Sensing he had been led to a very revealing path, with a smile of gratitude and sure movement the young man thanked the 21st Century Bodhisattva and took his leave.

-- Am stopping my finger now, thank you for reading.
(6.3.14)

The Natural Face

There is a traditional adage that says if one lives in a place long enough, and in mindful manner gets out into the wildness of that place, that resident "energies" will make themselves known and help guide that person, via awakened notions and insights, to more intimately "know" not only that place but, by extension, the infinite network of all places.

Deep in the rugged forest canyons of the Pacific Northwest, far from even the most remote logging roads, people live. Some are in small groups, many are alone, living in practical, self-built structures, eating what is available to them. Grounded deeply within themselves and the surrounding wilderness, they are believed to live lives that are impartially, relentlessly and beautifully free.

. . .

I have heard stories of a man, apparently somewhat odd in his ways, who lives on a small ridge overlooking a creek near the bottom of a particularly deep watershed ravine, a man who is said to be a deeply awakened Buddhist practitioner, perhaps even a burgeoning Buddha.

The stories say he is usually accommodating to hikers who happen upon his camp, once he sizes them up and determines responsible intentions. And, people relate, he has for years apparently been partial to visitors who come in morning time, when the sun of the southeastern sky shines upon his ridge-top.

So it was early one morning I set out, driving east into the Cascades, up and over the Stevens Pass, and found the paved road that led to the dirt road that dead-ended in a clearing surrounded by deep underbrush, from which a switched-back trail descended into the steep canyon, ending at the creek that led to the man's camp.

The sun had broken over the forest canopy. After about an hour's walk along the creek-bed a glinting up ahead caught my eye. As I approached, I saw it was sunlight reflecting on the shoulders of a golden-colored Buddha statue, sitting atop a huge granite boulder. In the near distance I heard the Heart Sutra being chanted in a full-toned man's voice. I had arrived.

I waited in silence for a minute or so after the chanting stopped, and as I was about to call out hello I saw him standing on the ledge ahead, smiling, beckoning me to come join him.

I introduced myself, he did not tell me his name but shook my hand. Noticing the red protection cord around my neck, he chuckled and said, "Mahayana, eh? Which tradition?"

I told him the Gelugpa, and he nodded. "OK, Drakpa," he said, "I don't have a lot of time today but come on and sit down, drink some tea with me." From that moment he never referred to me other than as Drakpa, Losang Drakpa being the ordination name of Lama Tsongkhapa, the founder of the Gelug school of Tibetan Buddhism.

He had a deeply humble character, confidently kind and gentle and very quick witted. We talked about many things, ranging from a little about ourselves and the life-affirming warmth of morning sun to the benefit of Heart Sutra recitations ("keeping its message in mind makes everything one does a Dharma-infused activity," he said).

After about 40 minutes he looked at his watch and said he needed to be going in a few minutes as he had promised to help some down-creek friends with work they were doing.

Curious, I asked how living out here, far away from so much, resonated with his Dharma practice.

He sat quietly for a few moments, took a large sip of tea, and began explaining.

"Well, my friend Drakpa, it was many years ago, not too long after I began my Buddhist inquiries, that I realized that the framework of Dharma studies and practices was, in the largest sense, an ecological one . . . devoted to asserting and nurturing the rights and well-being of all beings in our environment, not just human ones.

"And clear to see, running through that ecology are the threads and intersections of impermanence and place. In this life, which doesn't occur for very long, we can only be in one place at any point in time, and it has been my view that being deeply rooted in place is resonant with best recognizing and navigating the impermanence of all there is.

"So, as a devoted practitioner with 'science of life' inklings, seeking a suitable location in which to fully experience and live in accord with creatures of all shapes and sizes and life-spans, I went searching, and found this ridge.

"Living modestly in this wild place ... having traded the normal cultural 'must haves' and distractions for the natural creature 'comforts' that are so abundant here, my name and personal history are completely irrelevant. There are no entanglements interfering with breaking down boundaries and nurturing instinctive -- and fiercely rewarding -- selflessness, born of undeniable interconnection and innate sanity.

"Perceptions of inside and outside, my self and my surroundings, all is porous and transparent ... and everything ... look around at the rock and the trees, the flowing water and sunlight and morning fogs ... smell the flourishing life of the forest ... and the creatures, all the creatures ... as they and I share this wild place together each of them becomes an inextricably part of my being ... and I of theirs.

"Each year I return from the city ... arriving in early Spring and remaining until the nighttime freezing temperatures of the late Fall.

"I abide here in simple routine. I am nothing unique or special, I merge and unite ... steadfastly mindful to accord harmoniously as just another aspect of it all ... no more, no less. I've my books, writings and practice ... and everything I do honors and observes the well-being of the life forms with which I share this forest.

"My teacher calls this way of living 'Wearing the Natural Face'. . ."

Growing quiet, he gazed down toward the water and then up into the trees. I listened to the sounds of the creek: cold, clear mountain water rushing over rocks and stones.

He continued, "I'm well in body and happy in mind. I eat plainly, rise with the morning light and sleep when darkness falls. And I have many close friends and neighbors here among the water, land and air critters. We share in the food ... I talk, chant and sing to them regularly ..."

"In concert with this is meditation, the deepest of my individual practices. This is where the glorious connections between mind and body are recognized and magnified, and the intuitive oneness that blossoms is embraced and carried out to the surroundings, infusing everything I do.

"You see Drakpa, this forest, this ridge-top, is a microcosm of all that is. At each moment, we and our world are occurring with and within each other ... all locales, all people, all beings, all things ... empty of separateness, of unique individualism. We're all moving through this together ... each in our own place, sharing in the ongoing impermanence. To know this -- to really know it -- is indestructible preciousness, and to engage and live it then becomes a blessing for all, including our selves."

A pause for reflection, then, "Awareness of this is practice; my enduring way of navigating the Buddhist path."

With this he finished his tea and stood, signaling an end to our time together.

"I appreciate the tea and your time, the energies of this place dance very well with you, and you with them," I said gratefully. "It has been so very nice to meet you."

"Thanks Drakpa, it's been nice to meet you too, I'm glad you came by. Enjoy your time in the forest, where there's always so much to learn, and feel free to return here as you'd like."

"Thank you, I'll be sure to. And when I do, is there anything you'd like me to bring, anything you could use?"

A hearty laugh. "Oh, thanks Drakpa, that's OK, I've got everything I need . . . but if you'd like, feel free to bring along some nice bodhicitta, the seed of pure well-being . . . even in this fertile place there can never be too much of it."

As we shook hands he leaned in, kissed my cheek and said goodbye.

-- Am stopping my finger now, thank you for reading. (8.12.15)

The Last Yeti

The morning dawned cold and foggy high in the Khumbu Himalayan region of northeastern Nepal.

The old Yeti, the planet's last remaining member of the species referred to locally as "the man things of the snows" and in Western huckster-speak as the Abominable Snowman, sat alone at the entrance of his small cave, hidden behind piles of large boulders and immense wild rhododendron bushes.

Aware of an unusually grim wind swooping through the narrow canyon, and sensing that his and the surrounding mountains would soon stir and vibrate and perhaps shift as never before, the Yeti decided to bring some food inside the cave and wait out what was to come.

The day is Saturday, April 25, 2015. Unknown to the Yeti, what was approaching would bring with it his -- and therefore his entire species' -- final moments of existence.

. . .

Most Nepalis do not have first-hand experiential evidence that the Yeti exists, they know only what's been said in the stories they've heard. And almost every Nepali has heard a Yeti story or two.

Some of the details in these narratives are outrageous, including those describing one physical feature that the Sherpas, inhabitants of the Khumbu Valley, often mention. This is the Yeti's backward feet, i.e., toes that point away from the direction in which it is walking, a deception it has developed to mislead those hunting it.

Yeti legends and tales abound among the people of the high Himalayas.

The Tibetan word for Yeti is "Me-Tay" -- herein we will use that name interchangeably with Yeti.

The Me-Tay reportedly moves very quickly, able to outrun a human, and lives high -- above 10,000 feet -- in the craggy Himalayas. They are said to be hairy and reddish-brown, with a ridged crown that projects a pointed-head appearance.

Yetis have reportedly been seen topping off at approximately ten feet tall, walking on either two or four feet, and they are apparently super-strong. There are stories of Yetis hoisting over their shoulder captured 1,500 pound yaks. Due to the altitude in which they live, sightings and encounters are usually reported by Himalayan yak and sheep herders.

Over the years, photographs and casts of Yeti footprints have been consistent -- what we see are very oddly broad primate feet. Reports of sightings, most of which come from the populous Sherpa country of northeastern Nepal, are also alike in their descriptions.

The mountain people tell stories of Me-Tay aggression, attacking grazing animals by rolling boulders down upon them, causing stampedes and then carting off the slowest prey.

Yetis were apparently once numerous in the Khumbu, but herders tending to livestock set out poisoned barley to keep them from raiding their herds, killing many of them. Sherpa and Tibetan elders speak of there being dead Yetis everywhere.

There are also accounts of the Me-Tay bringing food to cave-dwelling monastic retreatants unable to get out to gather or receive food from nearby neighbors due to extreme winter climate.

The most common incidences of Yeti awareness occur at night, when frightening screams echo through the cold Himalayan canyons, driving villagers indoors. Through the years many people, including Westerners, have heard these wailing screeches, describing them similarly, the wild yelps reportedly sounding like increasingly shrill "Kak-kak-kak-KAI-ee . . ."

Tibetans tend to accept a hereditary connection between the Yetis and their Buddhist faith. Legend has it that a monkey with Buddhist sensibilities lived as a hermit in the mountains and was loved by and married a demoness; their offspring were born with long hair and tails, these being the source of the "man-things" of the snows, i.e., the Me-Tay. (How interesting, the basic similarity between this notion and our understandings of primate-to-human evolution.)

Sherpas also historically consider the Yetis to be fearless guardians of Dolma (Tara), the feminine aspect of Chenrezig, the radiant Buddhist representation of the perfectly compassionate mind.

• • •

Consider that for the people of the Himalayas the lines between physical and supernatural are not as narrow or solid as for us in the West.

Whether spirit or real animal, certainly there has been much skepticism concerning the existence of the Yeti due to the fact that expeditions in pursuit of them have repeatedly failed.

But what many do seem to agree upon is that in the steep rugged terrain of the Himalayas there is some creature; mysterious and unknown to science, that has existed for generations.

Until this fateful Saturday morning.

• • •

Earthquake. As the shaking intensified just before noon, a 75-by 37-mile section of Nepal violently shifted northward in excess of 10 feet in a matter of seconds. The earthquake -- Nepal's most severe in almost a century -- leveled villages far and near to the epicenter, caused deadly landslides and avalanches, crippled transportation networks and ended the lives of untold beings.

High in the Khumbu, the aged Me-Tay knew something was severely wrong. There had been many tremors and avalanches in the past, but this was different. The rumble was deafening and came from very deep within the mountain ... the cave walls were cracking and moving as though they were liquid.

Then a sharp boom, thunder-like, and in the next moment the Himalayan cave, fractured by the same geological elements that long ago created it and the mysterious mountains in which it was hidden, ceased to exist.

Huddled for safety in a corner of his long-time home, the last Yeti on Earth never felt the mountain crushing him as the roof above him disintegrated.

For him there was no fear, no horror, no pain ... only the experience of darkness ... timeless, safe and comforting in its expansiveness.

And then, as was happening for so many beings suddenly dead in the quaking canyons and valleys below, a pathway of clear light began to appear in the deepest recesses of his newly-freed mind ...

-- Am stopping my finger now, thank you for reading. (4.29.15)

www.ingramcontent.com/pod-product-compliance
Lightning Source LLC
Chambersburg PA
CBHW071918290426
44110CB00013B/1404